Praise for *Moving the Needle*

"Joe's game plan in *Moving the Needle* will help you on the road from success to significance."

—**Bob Buford**, author of *Half Time*

"Joe's program titled Operation Crossover, which he used his training for the U.S. Navy SEALs, taught me how to transition from military to civilian life. He has been a huge help to me personally and my fellow brothers in the SEAL teams. Joe helped me set a clearly defined goal for what I want next and helped me better understand how to put myself out there in the corporate world. With Joe's help, I have made a successful transition from the SEALs to General Motors by using the principles in *Moving the Needle*."

—**Patrick Bisher**, GM Group Leader, Production;
former Navy SEAL

"Joe's address to our leadership group at CUNA Mutual was a moving and inspirational experience for our team. He knows how to coach, lead, and inspire leaders."

—**Bob Trunzo**, President of CUNA Mutual Group Insurance &
Financial Services

"Joe Sweeney recently presented an inspirational keynote and workshop to our LexisNexis Women Connected group, which gave participants the tools to create game changers in their business and personal lives. Joe caused a powerful and positive paradigm shift for many who attended the workshop."

—**Louise Jones, JD**, LexisNexis, Process Improvement
Director—Customer Systems,
North American Research Solutions

"One percent of the people in the world do what they say they will do. One percent of the people in the world give without expectation of return. One percent of the people of the world understand how to connect with people by being a value provider. Joe Sweeney is in the 1 percent bracket. He has set the standard for doing business ethically and enthusiastically. I heartily recommend that you buy *Moving the Needle* and hire Joe to inspire your people to greater heights."

—**Jeffrey Gitomer**, best-selling author, keynote speaker, and sales authority

"Joe's book reveals key concepts for getting clear, free, and making significant improvements in your professional and personal life."

—**John Assaraf**, *New York Times* best-selling author of *The Answer* and *Having It All*, featured in the Blockbuster movie, *The Secret*

"*Moving the Needle* will help you to understand that we have been given a tremendous gift of longevity in our lives. Joe provides many tools for you to make the most out this most precious gift of time."

—**Ken Dychtwald, PhD**, author of *A New Purpose: Redefining Money, Family, Work, Retirement and Success*

"Over the years I've worked with Joe on various investment opportunities and have shared the principles from his book with my teams across the globe. Each and every time, Joe has added significant value to the process by providing simple, yet impactful insights that cause you to stop and reframe how you are approaching a project. Over the years nothing has impressed me more about Joe than what a great father he has been to his four children. To me, nothing tells you more about a person and his principles than how he treats and interacts with his family."

—**Mark Pacchini**, former President of Foote Cone & Belding Advertising; current CEO of rVue, Inc.

"Joe was helpful when he talked to our coaching staff during our NCAA Final Four run. Many of the concepts in *Moving The Needle* helped our team get to the Final Four in Dallas."

—**Bo Ryan**, Head Coach of the University of Wisconsin–Madison Badgers men's basketball team

"Joe Sweeney has "moved the needle" for my students at the University of Minnesota each time he has visited. This book captures his message of why and how to get clear, get free, and get going. Students of all ages can benefit from his game plan."

—**Joel Maturi**, Retired Director of Athletics, Current Instructor, University of Minnesota

"I strongly believe in the principles found in the following four books, so much so that I require all my employees to read them and am now adding a fifth—*Moving the Needle*.
The Intelligent Investor by Benjamin Graham
The Power of Positive Thinking by Norman Vincent Peale
How to Win Friends & Influence People by Dale Carnegie
Networking Is a Contact Sport by Joe Sweeney"

—**Ab Nicholas**, CEO of the Nicholas Company

"Joe's address to more than 400 Army Reserve soldiers, many with extensive deployment experience, significantly helped them maintain balance in their lives as citizen soldiers. Joe was a game changer for our troops."

—**Brigadier General John C. Hanley**, Commander, 3rd Battle Command Training Brigade, 75th Battle Command Training Division

"I have watched the concepts of the Winning Game Plan be implemented with many companies over the years and employ them often in my current role at Turtle Wax. The system works by creating positive daily changes in your professional and personal life."

—**Mark Leopold**, CEO of Turtle Wax Inc.

"Last fall Joe implemented the Winning Game Plan with our commercial banking team. It was so successful that we asked him to come back this year and repeat the program with our retail bankers. The program has made a real difference in the professional and personal lives of our employees."

—**Jay Mack**, President and CEO of Town Bank

"*Moving the Needle* is a playbook to be used by the health care industry. Getting clear, free, and going is the foundation for untangling the complexity that exists today and creating a future of more affordable, accessible, and higher-quality care. Joe Sweeney does it again."

—**Greg Borca**, national health care entrepreneur

"Reading *Networking Is a Contact Sport* and *Moving the Needle* were watershed moments in my career. Five years ago, I never would have believed that I could be in a business development role at my firm. Understanding your approach to sales and implementing the 5/10/15 program helped transform my daily routine. Your insights helped me to see that in my business, wealth management, networking, and sales are all about understanding people's needs and helping them find the right solution.

—**John V. Celentani**, Northern Trust

"*Moving the Needle* will help you and your team become the best version of yourselves."

—**Matthew Kelly**, *The New York Times* bestselling author of *The Dream Manager*

"Joe Sweeney's approach to improving personal performance is spot on. In both business and on the race track, the competitive set is fierce. You have to move the needle, or you will be left behind."

—**Mike Welsh**, Vice President, Commercial Development, Rahal Letterman Lanigan Racing; Former Director, Sports and Event Marketing, Miller Brewing Company

MOVING THE NEEDLE

MOVING THE NEEDLE

GET CLEAR, GET FREE, AND GET GOING IN YOUR CAREER, BUSINESS, AND LIFE

JOE SWEENEY
WITH MIKE YORKEY

WILEY

Contents

SECTION I Get Clear

SECTION II Get Free

Foreword

When I was in the major leagues, I played for the San Diego Padres, New York Yankees, California Angels, Toronto Blue Jays, Minnesota Twins, and Cleveland Indians from 1973–1995 and reached the pinnacle of performance, including the All-Star team for a dozen of those years.

I crossed paths with literally hundreds of sports icons and business personalities over the years. These meetings and interactions gave me insight on how to better myself and my performance as I learned something from many of them. The wisdom from my composite experiences helped me become a communicator through print, radio, and speaking platforms as well.

One of those people I learned from was Mark McCormack, a Cleveland lawyer who was instrumental in establishing the field of Sports Marketing. He started negotiating contracts and managing the careers of golf's Big Three: Arnold Palmer, Jack Nicklaus, and Gary Player. His company, International Marketing Group (IMG), grew to represent athletes from every professional sport, including Major League Baseball.

Because of my thirst for knowledge and personal and professional improvement, I picked up Mark's fascinating book, *What They Don't Teach You at Harvard Business School*. The basic thrust of the book was to teach you to read people, create the right first impression, and run meetings well. Many of his concepts were based on common-sense street smarts and a get-it-done attitude. For me, it was a must-read.

Mark McCormack is no longer with us today, but I know someone who reminds me a lot of him. After meeting through a mutual business group, Joe Sweeney has become a good friend of mine over the years. I've personally seen and experienced Joe's knack for combining his love of business and his passion for sports as part of his multifaceted career. He and I agree that the common element in these endeavors is our ability to network, connect, and communicate with others.

Joe's latest book, *Moving the Needle*, is a collection of tools, insights, and experiences rolled into a system of what works in the business and sports worlds. This book reminds me of *What They Don't Teach You at Harvard Business School* because it is filled with many of the same common-sense approaches to business and dealing with people. Sports provide a playground for life, and the lessons learned on the sports field can be readily implemented in all aspects of our daily lives. Joe's concepts are really about creating a practical system to improve human performance. *Moving the Needle* is about how to bring your A-game to your endeavors.

I played professional baseball for 22 years, where there are 162 games a year—and more with playoffs and the World Series. To reach the top, I had to prepare for all of those 2,973 regular season and 26 postseason games I played in: pitch by pitch, offense to defense, inning by inning, game by game, and year to year. Although I displayed peak performance quite often, the only constant was the playing of the National Anthem. Each game unfolded differently.

Performing well is not always easy, but with the correct system and discipline, you can work to be your best every day and avoid those huge performance fluctuations that people call "slumps." You can be sure that I've used many of these tools outlined in *Moving the Needle* to help me be my best on the field, in the boardroom, and in life.

Last, it's Joe's contention, and one I wholeheartedly agree with, that too many people are "stuck" these days and not moving forward in life. If you've ever thought that you needed a system to provide clarity about what you want to do and where you want to go in your career, in business, or in life, then you've come to the right place. Let *Moving the Needle* lead you in the right direction.

—Dave Winfield,
Hall of Fame Major League Baseball Player

Acknowledgments

To my parents, Ray and Marian Sweeney—who taught all of their 10 children that moving the needle wasn't about being better than anybody else, but being the best version of yourself, and that you had to work on this every day.

To my wife, Tami—the kindest and most caring woman I know, who gave me the freedom to pursue my passions.

To my four children, Kyle, Conor, Kelly, and Brendan and their significant others—who remind me on a daily basis of what is important and give me the why to keep going.

To my friends and wingmen—who have kept me on track and given me clarity when I needed it most.

To Sister Camille Kliebhan, OSF, for her grace, beauty, and wisdom and for teaching me that every day is full of grace-filled moments.

To the men and woman of our military, and especially the friends at the Navy Special Warfare Center in Coronado, California, for making the ultimate sacrifice—your lives—to protect our freedoms and liberties. Thank you for showing me how to be constantly grateful and to make every day count.

To the many teachers and mentors who have provided the tools and insights to help us get clear, get free, and get going in our businesses, careers, and lives.

And especially to Mike Yorkey, Colleen Heffron, and Shannon Vargo, who made *Moving the Needle* possible.

Introduction

Why This Book?

> It matters not whether we live up to the expectations
> of our fathers, but rather, we as fathers, live up to the
> expectations of our children.
>
> —SAMUEL C. JOHNSON, author of
> *Reflections of Lake Owen*

Is there a moment in time you can look back on and recognize that fate, Divine Providence—or whatever you want to call it—steered you in a certain direction and changed your life?

That happened to me. Four years ago, I was in downtown St. Paul, Minnesota, hanging out in a spacious condo atop the Saint Paul Hotel. The residence belonged to my good friend Craig Leipold, the owner of the Minnesota Wild National Hockey League team.

We were killing time before walking to the Xcel Energy Center for the start of the Minnesota Wild game. A green leather-bound book on the coffee table caught my eye. The title was *Reflections of Lake Owen,* and the author was Samuel C. Johnson, who was Craig's father-in-law and the patriarch of a family company that bore his name and made consumer products, including Johnson Wax, Windex glass cleaner, and Ziploc bags. The book was some type of memoir.

I sat down on the couch and flipped open to the first few pages. Johnson's words from the prologue hit me like a dump load of snow from a full Zamboni.

"My dear grandchildren" is how the prologue began. What followed were the words he hoped his grandchildren would read some day. After wishing he could protect them from the pains and hurts that would surely happen in life, he said that unfortunately, there was nothing he could do after he was gone, which is why he wanted to share his advice and lessons on life in the form of a book.

His words and insights resonated with me and inspired me to do the same for my family. This was exactly what I wanted to do for my children and grandchildren—to teach them the lessons I had learned in life.

After flying back to my hometown of Milwaukee, Wisconsin, I couldn't get Johnson's message out of my head. I had to share the lessons I'd learned in life with my children. Having never written a book in my life, I wasn't about to produce a 200-page memoir like Johnson did, so I settled on 14 one-page chapters. Each chapter had a message and a moral to it.

A few weeks later, I was having dinner with a few of my close friends at a downtown Milwaukee restaurant. These were the guys I could trust implicitly and whose advice I respected. They wanted to know how things were since our youngest child, Brendan, went off to college.

"Well, I've written a book," I joked, choosing not to tell them it was only 14 pages long. My buddies asked to hear more, so I shared what I did and some of the lessons I learned.

My friend Mark Pacchini slapped his hand on the table and said, "That's a book people should read. You could help so many."

I was flattered that Mark would say that. He ran the ad agency Foote, Cone & Belding in Chicago—it represented international corporations, including Boeing, KFC, Kraft Foods, Taco Bell, and the MillerCoors brewing company.

"What you have to say could help CEOs, sales organizations, college students, and members of the military coming back from the service," he said. "You should publish it."

I was pleased that Mark had faith in me. He believed my business background and life experiences could translate into a powerful business tool to benefit others. I was an investment banker with Corporate Financial Advisors in Milwaukee, but during my nearly 30 years in business, my favorite times were those spent consulting, speaking, and training. Over the years, I have been a businessman, an entrepreneur who bought and sold companies, as well as a sports agent for NFL players, baseball players, and golfers.

So I took the plunge. I worked with Mike Yorkey, a Southern California writer, to get the prose right. The result was *Networking Is a Contact Sport,* which was released in 2010. I learned early on that the relationships I made while running my business were more valuable than any ad campaign, cost-saving initiative, or product launch. The art of truly connecting with another—and all that entails—can at once be the simplest, most complex, and most rewarding talents one can endeavor to develop. We are trained in how to use systems, how to prepare presentation decks, and how to negotiate contracts, yet we are never taught how to engage, connect, or build a network. I wanted to write a book that would help others in business overcome insecurities, learn more effective networking skills, and establish deep, loyal, and meaningful relationships.

The message resonated so much that I developed a *Networking Is a Contact Sport* workshop and workbook that showed people how, through a series of exercises, they could actually develop skills to be better at building relationships. After attending my networking workshops, people asked me whether I had anything else that could help their teams operate at this elevated level in other aspects of their roles. "Can you help move the needle at our company and improve our overall performance?" the managers asked.

Hearing their requests got me thinking again. Was there a need for an in-depth, ongoing training program that focused on business and personal development? There had to be because when business leaders were asking me whether I had anything else to share, what they were really asking was this:

"Can you help us change human behavior?"

Part of what has made me so interested in the field of networking has been my insatiable curiosity about what makes people tick. People love sharing what motivates them or makes them behave in a certain way; showing interest in learning about them creates an instant bond. Here are two questions I always ask people I meet:

Why do you do what you do in life?

Why have you made the decisions you've made?

So, when dozens of business leaders approached me about what other programs I had in the works, I asked more questions. The leaders told me they were not looking just for motivation or inspiration. They wanted to know how they could improve their performance as well as that of their employees.

Invariably, three issues consistently popped up. Whether they were business leaders, managers, employees, teachers, or parents, they all reported having a hard time with:

- Getting clear
- Getting free
- Getting going

This observation applied to their professional, as well as their personal, lives. They were glued to the ground, unsure of the path they should take or whether they had the freedom to move forward. They weren't getting anywhere, be it in life, in business, or in relationships. In other words, they couldn't get clear, get free, or get going to achieve their goals.

Because of what the marketplace was saying, I decided to write *Moving the Needle* and share a collection of innovative tools that I've used over the past several decades to help me get clear, get free, and get going. To ensure the lessons of this book are adopted, I also developed a 52-week program to help people get clear, get free, and get going. (You can find out more about the 52-Week Winning Game Plan for Business and Personal Development in the back of the book. If you don't have 52 weeks to get going, this program can be adapted to shorter times, such as 16 weeks or 8 weeks.)

That said, *Moving the Needle* is about changing human behavior. For example, if you want to lose 50 pounds, I could help you accomplish that goal, as I've done with a few close friends. Much like changing behavior after reading a book or listening to a 1-hour keynote is challenging, losing 50 pounds after 1 hour in the gym is just as difficult. That's why I have developed a program to help you change behaviors.

So ask yourself:

- Am I stuck?
- Am I having a hard time figuring out what I want to do next in my career?
- Have I recently experienced a change or unforeseen event that forced me to rethink my plans for the future?
- Do I know how to move forward from where I am right now?
- Do I have a game plan and an end goal in sight?

When I talk about getting clear, getting free, and getting going—the mantra of this book—I've found that often people have achieved one or two of these goals but not all three. For instance, you may be clear about what you want to do and actually be progressing toward that goal, but you don't feel free. You may be free to embark on a path of your choosing or to change your course, but you're not clear about your goals and aspirations. To live a fulfilling life, you need to understand all three of these principles.

The issue people most commonly cite when I ask them what is holding them back is a lack of clarity. They might be successful in their careers or feeling free because they have their own company, but they're not clear on where they should be going next. When I coach people, I ask, "What does success look like to you? Starting your own company? Doubling sales in the next year? Spending more time at home?"

I don't know, Joe. I just want to get up every day and do a good job and be successful.

These days, that's not enough. What you're going to learn about in *Moving the Needle* is how you can get clear so that you can get free and get going. After I break down each directive, I'll guide you through a series of short exercises at the end of each chapter so that you'll be pointed in the right direction. You'll find that everything works logically, but you'll need to study each chapter and thoughtfully respond to the questions to get the most out of this book.

I urge you to see this through. The principles are meant to be tenets you incorporate into your life each day. It will be fun to challenge yourself to move the needle and make improvements or a key transition in life.

Moving the Needle is for anyone looking to get better in his or her career, business, or life. It doesn't matter who you are or what stage of life you're in. You may be a college student, a returning military veteran, an intern trying to get a foot in the door, an account executive stuck in middle management, an entrepreneur wondering how to grow a business, or a CEO trying to turn around a sad-looking balance sheet. Each one of you will be on your way to get clear, get free, and get going by the time you finish *Moving the Needle*.

After working with world-class athletes and successful executives for decades, one thing is clear: *What people can achieve is nothing short of astonishing, but to deliver extraordinary results consistently requires coaching.* That is where this book comes in.

Moving the Needle is designed to help you define your goals, focus your efforts, and give you the tools you need to create a system that will help you not only establish, but also maintain clarity, freedom, and motivation.

When I have employed the tools and systems in this book, my life has become richer and fuller and blessed with experiences, purpose, and meaning. *And so can yours.* My hope is that you use this book and employ these systems to get clear, get free, and get going and to make game changers a daily experience. Have fun with this, and find some friends to share these exercises with you.

A Closing Thought

After watching and studying athletes and successful executives for decades, I have concluded that nobody plays consistently at a high level without coaching.

—Joe Sweeney

Get Clear

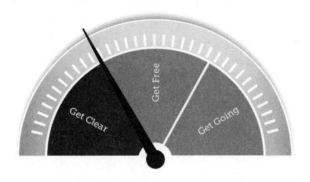

Get clear, get free, and get going.

Of these three simple directives, getting clear—defined here as having clarity of mind and striving with a sense of purpose—is the most important and the toughest to do. Maintaining perspective on business and life is a skill that takes decades to master, if it's mastered at all.

Identifying what's most important to you and what isn't is fundamental to getting clarity. If you don't take these steps to determine what's key in your life, then you'll be unsure and unclear about where you should be going or what you should be doing.

Often, people who are unclear focus on the details of day-to-day life because they're unable to concentrate on long-term goals. When you aren't sure what you truly want to do or are afraid to pursue it, paralysis sets in. Many fall into a state of stasis and wait for opportunities to come along, but this means they settle on whatever opportunities come their way rather than seeking out favorable moments that are right for them. One thing successful people have in common is an absolute sense of mission—at all costs.

As you read this section, think about what matters most to you, what you're doing that detracts or distracts from that, and what it would take to get rid of the clutter in your life and get clear. Once you identify and acknowledge the goals that are most important to you—and identify the obstacles to them, whether real or imagined, self-imposed, or forced on you—you will begin to have clarity and a sense of purpose about the future. Better yet, you'll feel much more confident about the direction you're heading.

CHAPTER 1

When It Comes to Getting Clear, First Get Quiet

Get Clear

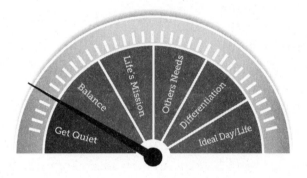

The monotony and solitude of a quiet life stimulates the creative mind.

—ALBERT EINSTEIN, twentieth-century physicist

If you're not sure where you're going in life or feel like you're not going anywhere, think back to your childhood when you played hide-and-seek and concealed yourself in a bedroom closet full of clothes. Inside that dark closet, while you waited for one of your friends or siblings to discover you, you had to be quiet and not make a sound. Your eyes and ears adjusted to your surroundings—the darkness, stillness, and silence. All that was left was getting lost in your thoughts or your imagination.

So what happened in the closet as you got quiet? Your eyes adjusted to the darkness and your senses were heightened. You were quiet because you *had* to be quiet.

Finding time to get quiet, get focused, and get lost in our thoughts or imagination is considered a luxury to most today. We spend our days with smartphone buds in our ears, listening to calls while our thumbs rush to compose e-mails as we run between the day's meetings, which usually leave us running late for our evening's social functions or family dinner. Sound familiar?

If so, here's my number one rule for getting clear, which is to *get quiet*. When you get quiet, you get clear enough to ask yourself, "What am I pursuing and why?" This is the most important question because many of us climb to the top of ladder only to discover that we're at the wrong house.

So, when was the last time you were quiet? It's probably been a while because of the influx of technological advances in the past 15 years—smartphones, iPads, Kindles, iPods, and MP3 players. Streaming movies, TV shows, and sporting events on our tablet computers and handheld devices have changed the definition of *downtime*. It used to be that we sat in a comfy chair and curled up with a book to recharge our batteries; now even downtime is spent furiously trying to keep up with a flood of e-mails and Facebook messages while working our way through a backlog of phone calls. Every waking hour, it's constant. There's no time to catch our collective breath.

The reason we're huffing and puffing is because we're too busy, which we've somehow associated with being productive. When we tell others that we're so busy, what we're really trying to do is subtly impress others with our self-importance. Brigid Schulte, author of *Overwhelmed: Work, Love, and Play When No One Has the Time*, says, "Somewhere around the end of the twentieth century, busyness became not just a way of life but a badge of honor. And life, sociologists say, became an exhausting everydayathon."[1]

If you're shopping on your smartphone while you're sitting on the toilet, you're too busy.

To get quiet, you could spend an unplugged weekend in total silence at a monastery, but that isn't realistic for most. Instead, carve out small windows of time to contemplate and reflect on where you've been and where you want to be. This time can also serve as a reset, where you close the books on details that have been weighing on you and start anew. Next, think about these questions, knowing that your answers may change over time:

1. Who are you? What defines you?
2. What is happening inside you?
3. What drives you?
4. What are your passions?
5. What are some things you can do today to get clear?

These five questions can help you be more present and aware of what direction your life is taking. Sometimes when you get quiet, you may not like what you see. Think of a lake where the wind has whipped up the waves, and you can't see below the surface. When it's calm and quiet, you can often see all the way to bottom—or at least see the fish swimming below the surface. You might spot tires and refuse on the bottom—and may not be pleased with what you see. That's okay. This is the first step in getting clarity. It takes time and commitment to truly get quiet, and once you do, you might be shocked at what you discover about yourself. Start by taking 10 minutes for self-reflection and see what you discover.

It Keeps Getting Faster and Faster

Technology is accelerating so fast that we don't have time to get clear. Consider this:

- It took radio 38 years to reach 50 million listeners.
- It took television 13 years to reach 50 million viewers.
- It took the Internet four years to reach 50 million users.
- It took Facebook one year to reach 50 million users.
- And it took smartphone apps just *nine months* to reach 50 million users.

It looks like instant gratification isn't fast enough anymore.

OUR OBSESSION WITH BUSYNESS

At what point did our obsession with busyness become a badge of honor? We seem to be consumed with cramming more in a day, in an hour, and in a minute than ever before. We thought technology would help us manage our busyness, but in reality, the opposite has transpired. The more time-saving gadgets and applications we have, the more we try to do. It seems counterintuitive, but the more time-saving technology we have, the less time we have.

Because of this—and many other things—we don't have any time to reflect or think about how we're living our lives. When we do take time to get quiet, we uncover the things in life that intrigue and inspire us, but more important, we learn to tune out some of the noise in our lives that doesn't matter. We learn to say *yes* to what is important and *no* to what is not.

Whenever I think about how busy we can get, I recall an amusing story about one of my brother's friends named Tom, who worked in the warehouse for a distribution company. He was a slight fellow who reminded everyone of Woody Allen.

Tom was eventually laid off from his job. My brother, Mark, would run into him from time to time and ask, "Hey, Tom, how are you doing?"

Tom had gone to work for a competitor, and he would say, "Oh, man, Mark. Let me tell you ... we are busy! Oh, how we are busy!"

These exchanges went on for a year or so:

"Tom, how are you doing?"
"Oh, Mark, man, are we busy!"

This went on until one time Tom said, "We're so busy that if we get any busier, they're going to have to move me to full time!"

Tom was busy all right. He was like many who've built barriers in their minds of what they can and cannot do. In Tom's mind, his definition of being busy was working part time.

Do you know people who can't stop talking about how busy they are? When you inquire *why* they're so busy, they usually respond with something like, "Well, I have to go to the store to pick up a few things, and then I have things to do around the house. Yes, it's going to be a very busy day," which prompted me to come up with a great title for my next book: *When You Have Nothing to Do, It's Hard to Get It All Done.*

If people think they have a busy day ahead, then they will have a very busy day—it becomes a self-fulfilling prophecy. That's not the road you want to take to get clear.

THE SOUND OF SILENCE

Getting quiet affords you the time to develop your instincts. Most people find they get into the most trouble both personally and professionally when their gut was telling them—screaming, even—to go in a different direction.

Instead, you plow ahead, not taking the time to think critically about your course of action. Instead of calling time-out, you keep the play clock going and rush into decisions that quickly turn south, much to your regret.

We've all made that same mistake. I've been consulting with a well-respected attorney—and a mother of two young children— who manages quite a workload because she's a top corporate lawyer, one of the best. When I asked her about taking time to reflect, she responded, "Joe, I don't even have time to go to the bathroom. I get up, get my kids ready, and run out the door. Everything's a rush."

Granted, we all have busy seasons of our lives, but no matter your schedule, workload, or obligations, try to make time to breathe, reflect, process, and plan at the beginning of the day. Even if you have only two minutes, you have to get quiet to get clear because quiet time clears the mind to perform at its optimal level.

"True silence is the rest of the mind; it is to the spirit what sleep is to the body: nourishment and refreshment," said William Penn, the first great hero of American liberty, who lived from 1644 to 1718. A thousand years before Penn, ancient philosopher Lao Tzu said, "Silence is a source of great strength."

Too few individuals tap into this source of strength or carve out quiet time during the course of their day. When asked if they incorporate quiet time into their routines, thousands of people from all walks of life, from business to education to military personnel, say the same thing: "There's just no time."

HAVE AN END GOAL IN MIND

Many of us don't have a plan for the future. Like chess players moving pawns around the board without thinking through the ramifications of bigger moves with the king and queen, we don't have the big picture in mind because we never sit down and think about the end goal.

> **Worth Repeating**
>
> You've got to be very careful if you don't know where you're going, because you might not get there.
>
> —Yogi Berra, former New York Yankees catcher

When it comes to getting clear, try to have a fixed goal in mind. Sure, people want to be promoted, start a business, develop the killer app, or make millions from the right investments, but when it comes to getting clear about your career and your life, you really have to identify your goal first. As New York Yankees catcher Yogi Berra famously quipped, "You've got to be very careful if you don't know where you're going, because you might not get there."

This six-step plan will help you on the path to getting clear.

1. Set Concise and Realistic Goals

Setting concise and realistic goals is difficult to do because zillions of thoughts compete for your attention every day. The National Science Foundation estimates that we have between 10,000 and 50,000 thoughts every 24 hours. More cerebral folks have a mind-boggling 60,000 thoughts a day.[2]

No doubt that's a tremendous amount of dialogue and random ideas running through our heads every second, hour, and day of our lives. There are also lots of clutter and negative thoughts—*You'll never get that done* or *You'll mess up*—muddying up our brains. Unfortunately for some people, those thoughts harden into concrete and become the story of who they are.

Don't let that happen to you. The key to identifying realistic goals is making sure they align with your overall objectives. Have you used a time of reflection to think through what you want and why you want it?

Sure, there have been times when I've regretted the decisions I've made. The direction I took led to a roadblock; other times, my best-laid plans blew up in my face. That happens to all of us, but that's how we learn—through experience.

What I often hear people say is that when they look back, they either didn't take enough time to get quiet and really listen to the small voice inside of them or they failed to set clear goals with an end in mind.

We are *kidnapped by the urgent*. We become so focused on imminent tasks and deadlines that we lose sight of the bigger picture of what we want to achieve. This is a pitfall that can affect both our personal and professional lives. It's critical to put what is important first when setting goals. Work diligently to make a daily practice of getting quiet. The clarity you will experience will be transformational.

2. Ask Why—Of Yourself and of Others

If you start asking yourself why you're doing the things you do—working toward a particular goal, taking a particular course of action, making certain decisions—that will help you better define your goals and values as well as help you make better decisions about where you should be focusing your time and efforts.

Many people, when setting a goal, say they want to be financially independent, which should prompt follow-up questions:

Why is that important to you?
Because I'd like a nice lifestyle.

And why is that important to you?

Because growing up, I didn't have any money, and I felt embarrassed and humiliated. There was a lot of pain in my family.

This is a common motivation, which is fine, but asking follow-up questions is like peeling back the layers of an onion. I remember a time when this happened with a business acquaintance who called me with a request. "Sweens, can you get me a pair of courtside seats to the Bucks game when the Miami Heat comes to town?" he asked over the phone.

I'm a member of the board of directors at the BMO Harris Bradley Center, where the Milwaukee Bucks of the National Basketball Association play their games. I don't have the pull to come up with courtside seats at the snap of my fingers, but I know where to make the right inquiries.

"Why do you want two courtside seats? They're pretty expensive," I asked this business associate.

The guy hesitated, "I have an important customer coming in."

"Really? Why do you want to take him to the game?"

"Oh, I don't know. I can impress him, show him that I'm a big guy around here."

"Why is this important to you?"

"If you really want to know, my dad died three years ago. The night before he died, I took him to a Bucks game. We had courtside seats, and I haven't been able to stop thinking about my last memory of my father."

I got it. His answer floored me, so I worked extra hard to get him his courtside seats. And he appreciated what I did for him. Asking why is a great tool to connect with people and help you get clear, not only with other people but also for yourself.

A lot of times when you ask why, people won't answer directly. Some will deflect the question, perhaps lie, or say what they think you want to hear. Keep asking questions anyway, albeit in a friendly manner, which will give you clarity about moving forward.

If you have a big enough *why,* the *how* will take care of itself. Of the six steps, this is the most important one because continuously asking why helps ensure our decisions and actions align with the course of action we are taking.

> **Food for Thought**
>
> If you have a big enough *why, the how* will take care of itself.

One client I worked with had a serious drinking problem. He told me that friends had asked him to tone down his drinking, but he hadn't been able to do so.

I searched for a question that would give him a big enough why.

"Do you plan to walk your daughter down the aisle on her wedding day?" I asked.

The man's face lit up. "Of course!" he exclaimed.

"I'm afraid if you don't get some help and quit drinking, there's a good chance that you'll be dead and gone before your daughter gets married."

Shortly after our conversation, he stopped drinking. He had created a big enough why to figure out how to make a major change in his life: to be around for his daughter's wedding day.

3. Don't Wait around for Something to Happen—Take Action

Life, it's been said, is a 24-hour white sale. You often have to act more quickly than you think. Knowing that, you don't have time to diddle-daddle.

It's like throwing your backpack over the wall first. You know what happens when you do that? That means you're all in. You're committed. Also, it's up to you to make it work.

After reading that, you may say, *I'm not ready to take that chance.*

We all fear change and the risks involved when making a bold move. The fear of the unknown and the fear of failure are enough to keep anyone from taking action. Dr. Wayne W. Dyer, author of *Wishes Fulfilled: Mastering the Art of Manifesting,* says if that's the case for you, then you need to adopt this attitude: *You cannot fail; you can only produce results. It's better to jump in with both feet and experience life than to stand on the sidelines, fearing that something might go wrong.*[3]

Nothing is perfect. Things *always* go wrong. So waiting until the conditions are perfect, the stars are aligned, or the funding is 100 percent in place before you take a chance rarely happens in real life. The sooner you realize that, the sooner you will be free of the fear that something will go wrong. There will never be a perfect time. Rather than spending time waiting for the ideal opportunity, use that time to thoughtfully consider the pros and cons *during* a time of reflection.

Whether you are unsure about how to take action or know exactly how to start, complete the Winning Action Plan at the end of this chapter to assist you in getting clear. The worksheet lists five categories:

- Business
- Personal
- Family
- Health
- Financial

Carve out a block of time to think them through. After defining your goals within each of the five categories, describe why you chose them, what action steps are required to make them happen, and what you're doing to see them through. Consider the pros and cons of each area. Identify the risks, consequences, and work involved in reaching the goals you set and what direction you will take in life.

4. Manage Momentum

I've worked with dozens of CEOs, vice presidents, businessmen, and businesswomen who got excited about a new initiative or direction in their companies, but two weeks later, any momentum they had fizzled.

You can best manage any momentum by securing support and surrounding yourself with people who, not only are on board with you, but also share your vision. Managing momentum leads to the fifth step, which is finding an accountability partner or partners to help keep you on task.

5. Secure Support by Building an Army around You

Do you ever notice when you set goals, you get excited, but your excitement levels off rather quickly? It's like when you sign up for a health club membership on January 2, but by the middle of February, you've lost your drive to exercise. If you had a workout buddy, however, you'd be far more likely to keep that 6:30 AM exercise appointment.

Your buddies or army are close friends or accountability partners who have your back. Another word for accountability partners is *wingmen*. Wingmen, who act as sounding boards, are part of your inner circle.

When you're trying to get clear, wingmen are those with listening ears who know you well and can see things you don't see. They give you vision and are pillars of support, but you have to be willing to hear what they have to say—and even invite them to share their opinions.

6. Last, Be Thinking about Game Changers

When it comes to moving the needle, sometimes you have to make bold moves. What could you do to shake things up?

SEE ALL OBSTACLES IN YOUR WAY

So, can you see clearly now?

That reminds me of a hit song from the early 1970s titled "I Can See Clearly Now" by Johnny Nash. Originally a pop-reggae hit, some may recognize it from the soundtrack of *Cool Runnings,* the 1993 film about the Jamaican bobsled team.

I can still hear the upbeat tempo in my head, but singer Johnny Nash may have been ahead of his time. In the recap below, I share steps you can take to get clear so that you can enjoy a bright, bright, sunshiny day.

As the great artist Michelangelo said, "The greater danger for most of us lies not in setting our aim too high and falling short, but in setting our aim too low and achieving our mark."

Joe's Recap

When It Comes to Getting Clear, First Get Quiet

Keep these thoughts in mind as you consider making some major changes:

- To get clear, it's important to get quiet.
- Realize that today's technology makes it almost impossible to get quiet. That means you'll have to act intentionally.
- Establish a morning routine that includes quiet reflective time. Start by spending 10 minutes each day in silence. If you can't find 10 minutes, start with 2 minutes.
- Try to turn off smartphone notifications and check your e-mails two or three times a day. You will become much more productive and free from distractions.
- Look for ways *not* to be so busy, which will greatly increase your opportunity to get clear.
- Remove clutter by taking care of 1- to 3-minute tasks immediately.
- Try to free up time for yourself by finding areas you can cut back on, such as watching TV and getting caught up on social media.
- Become aware. What do you eat, drink, think, and do? What are your favorite activities? With whom do you spend time?

- After you figure out what you want, create a big enough why.
- Manage the momentum on your journey by securing proper support.
- Be thinking about creating a game changer in your life. What's one thing you could do today or this week to shake things up?

Exercises

1. Do you currently take quiet time in your day? If not, where and when will you take time to pause and get quiet? _____

_____

_____

2. Fill out the Winning Action Plan. Create a goal for each of the following five categories. Start with an end in mind, asking *why* you have chosen this goal and listing the action steps needed to reach the goal. Think through how you will keep the momentum going and what support will be needed. Be sure to list in detail.

3. What would be a great game changer in your life? What steps do you need to take to make it happen?

_____

_____

_____

4. What do you need to say *no* to in your life to get clear?

_____

_____

_____

(continued)

(continued)

Winning Action Plan				
Goals	Why	Actions	Manage Momentum	Secure Support
1. Business	1.	1.		
	2.	2.		
	3.	3.		
	4.	4.		
	5.	5.		
2. Personal	1.	1.		
	2.	2.		
	3.	3.		
	4.	4.		
	5.	5.		
3. Family	1.	1.		
	2.	2.		
	3.	3.		
	4.	4.		
	5.	5.		
4. Health	1.	1.		
	2.	2.		
	3.	3.		
	4.	4.		
	5.	5.		
5. Financial	1.	1.		
	2.	2.		
	3.	3.		
	4.	4.		
	5.	5.		

FIGURE 1.1

CHAPTER **2**

Life Balance and the Life Decision Wheels

Get Clear

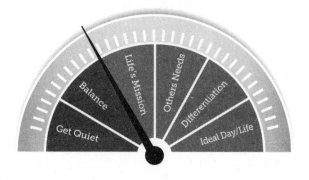

A true balance between work and life comes with knowing that your life activities are integrated, not separated.

—MICHAEL THOMAS SUNNARBORG, author of *21 Keys to Work/Life Balance: Unlock Your Full Potential*

When I talk about getting clear to audiences, I often see a forlorn expression on people's faces:

Joe, you don't know how overwhelmed I am.

It's a juggling act when it comes to managing a career, having an active social life, spending time with family and friends, and staying healthy. How can any of us get it all done?

Many can't. Balancing work and life was a clear problem for 89 percent of respondents to a survey conducted by StrategyOne, a global market research firm. Of 613 respondents, 54 percent identified it as a significant issue in their lives. With our roles in the workplace expanding, time with the family or significant others takes the brunt of the hit, followed by personal downtime. People are expected to be *always on*. Not only do technology advances make us more available, but reducing the size of the workforce also places even more pressure on employees. Many would say that technology has created the endless workday.

I liken the feat of achieving balance across the various demands most of us face to a famous segment from *The Ed Sullivan Show*. The performer's name was Erich Brenn, and he used to spin dinner plates on long reedlike poles. He would balance the first plate atop a pole, and with a few swift sweeps of the edge of the plate, he'd have the plate spinning precariously atop the thin pole. Plate after plate he'd start each one spinning, until a dozen plates were rotating in the air.

When one plate would start to slow and wobble, he'd dash to the unsteady plate and shake the stick just so, which would cause the plate to spin furiously again. It wasn't long before he was hopping from plate to plate to keep them going, which was the entertaining part. Could Erich Brenn keep his plates spinning in the air?

You might be asking yourself the same question. You race from one thing to the next, usually arriving just in time, but each cheek-puffing effort causes exertion and stress. So the question for you: How many plates do you have spinning in the air? How many times has one crashed to the floor?

To have many different plates spinning at once has become the default. The goal is to be aware of the different plates, to recognize the most important plates, and to keep the most precious plates spinning smoothly. When the number of plates you are spinning exceeds your ability to spin all the plates, life goes awry. If your plates are crashing into pieces, perhaps you have taken on too much or are losing focus on the things that matter most. It's hard to get clear and stay clear when this happens because your focus is on reactively managing tasks rather than proactively achieving goals.

What's spinning in your life right now? What are you facing in your career and life? Are your plates spinning smoothly? Are there plates crashing to the ground? Do you know where you're going?

FIGURE 2.1   How many plates do you have spinning?

Fostering a *creative awareness,* or mindfulness, about where you are, what you are doing, and where you are going is an important step in getting clear and having an organized and productive life—and keeping those plates spinning in the air. To help you develop a habit of being more mindful, first identify the key segments in your life, including the various activities, responsibilities, and demands you face. You may want to consider these eight areas:

1. *Career and job:* What do you do for a living? What would you like to be doing?
2. *Financial:* Are you thriving or just surviving on your salary?
3. *Relationships:* How would describe your social life? What are your relationships like? Are you happy with where you are?
4. *Health and fitness:* Are you carving out time to exercise and be healthy? Are you happy with where you are?
5. *Contribution:* It's been said that it's better to give than to receive. Is there a charity or cause to which you donate or volunteer time?
6. *Personal growth:* Have you taken any "me time" recently? How are you striving to improve yourself or burnish your skills? Are you a continuous learner?

7. *Spiritual growth:* Are you part of a church or faith community, and are you forming relationships with others? How important is the spiritual component of your life?

8. *Recreation:* What are you doing to get away? What do you like to do on weekends or vacation time?

Worth Considering

Do you find it interesting that so many of us lose our health in pursuit of money, only to spend the money we acquired to get our health back?

Once you identify and define the various aspects that make up your life, you can plug these into a hub-and-spoke system called the Life Decision Wheels (Figure 2.2). The key to great clarity and productivity is having the ability to segment the different areas of your life and approach each day in an organized and focused manner.

Take some quiet time to clear your mind and think about your life. Write specific action steps relating to each topic in the decision wheel. Your observations will give you a lot more clarity about the areas you're putting a lot of time and effort into and those areas that you're overlooking.

Look at how three people might fill out the wheels, based on their age and career development. The first is a 25-year-old male who graduated from a Big Ten school a couple of years ago with a business administration degree (Figure 2.3). He works at a midlevel firm as an inventory analyst. He is single, is juggling a bucketful of college loans, and owns a Siberian husky. He plays in a flag football league and skis with his buddies in the Colorado Rockies every February.

Next, see how the wheel looks for a 38-year-old female executive who's married with two children (Figure 2.4). She works for a major big-box retailer (think Target or Kmart) and oversees the buying for the young-teen area. She loves her position, which pays more than her husband's job as an English teacher at a public high school.

This is a baby boomer example—a 55-year-old woman who's an investment advisor with demanding clients and a tough boss (Figure 2.5). She's also known as a full-fledged member of the

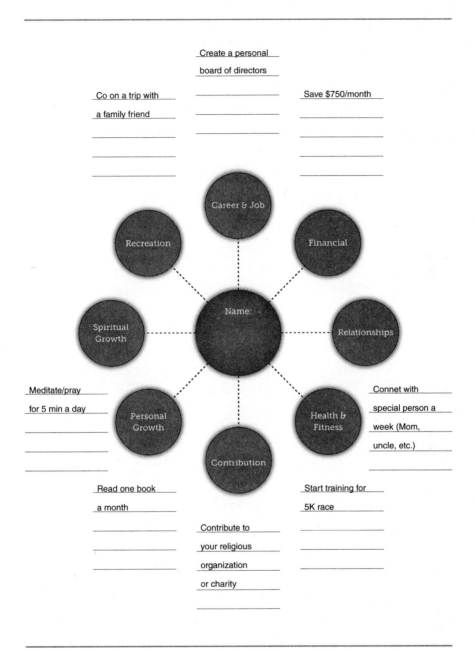

Create a personal
board of directors

Co on a trip with
a family friend

Save $750/month

Career & Job

Recreation

Financial

Name:

Spiritual
Growth

Relationships

Meditate/pray
for 5 min a day

Personal
Growth

Health &
Fitness

Connet with
special person a
week (Mom,
uncle, etc.)

Contribution

Read one book
a month

Start training for
5K race

Contribute to
your religious
organization
or charity

FIGURE 2.2   Sample Life Decision Wheels

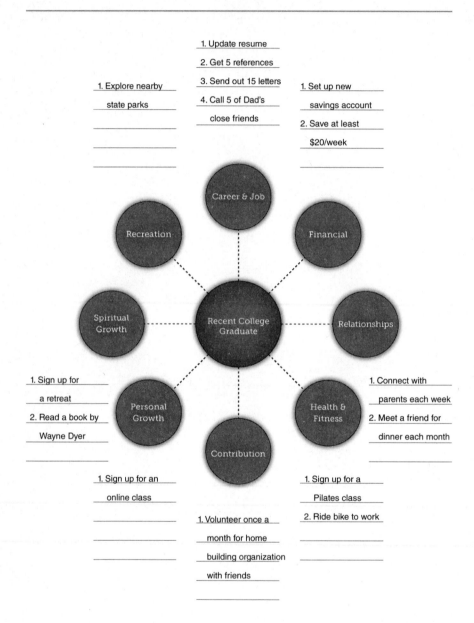

1. Update resume

2. Get 5 references

3. Send out 15 letters

4. Call 5 of Dad's

   close friends

1. Explore nearby

   state parks

1. Set up new

   savings account

2. Save at least

   $20/week

1. Sign up for

   a retreat

2. Read a book by

   Wayne Dyer

1. Connect with

   parents each week

2. Meet a friend for

   dinner each month

1. Sign up for an

   online class

1. Volunteer once a

   month for home

   building organization

   with friends

1. Sign up for a

   Pilates class

2. Ride bike to work

Career & Job

Recreation

Financial

Spiritual Growth

Recent College Graduate

Relationships

Personal Growth

Contribution

Health & Fitness

FIGURE 2.3 Life Decision Wheels for a Recent College Graduate

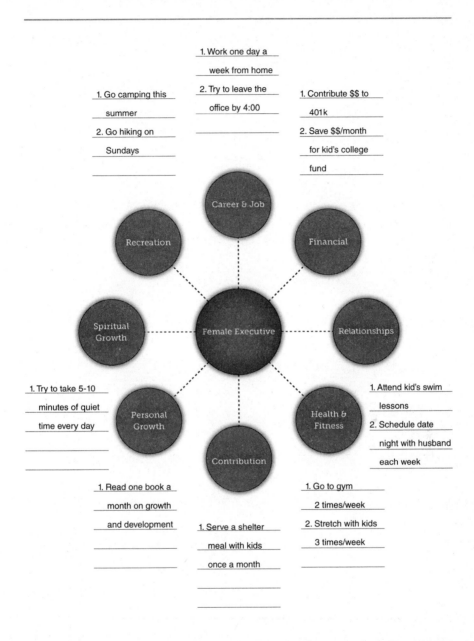

1. Work one day a
   week from home
2. Try to leave the
   office by 4:00

1. Go camping this
   summer
2. Go hiking on
   Sundays

1. Contribute $$ to
   401k
2. Save $$/month
   for kid's college
   fund

Career & Job

Recreation

Financial

Spiritual
Growth

Female Executive

Relationships

1. Try to take 5-10
   minutes of quiet
   time every day

Personal
Growth

Health &
Fitness

1. Attend kid's swim
   lessons
2. Schedule date
   night with husband
   each week

Contribution

1. Read one book a
   month on growth
   and development

1. Go to gym
   2 times/week
2. Stretch with kids
   3 times/week

1. Serve a shelter
   meal with kids
   once a month

FIGURE 2.4   Life Decision Wheels for a Female Executive

1. Cut back from
full time to
30 hours/week

1. Go on canoe trip
with a friend

1. Add $$/month to
retirement account
2. Meet with financial
planner and
update plans

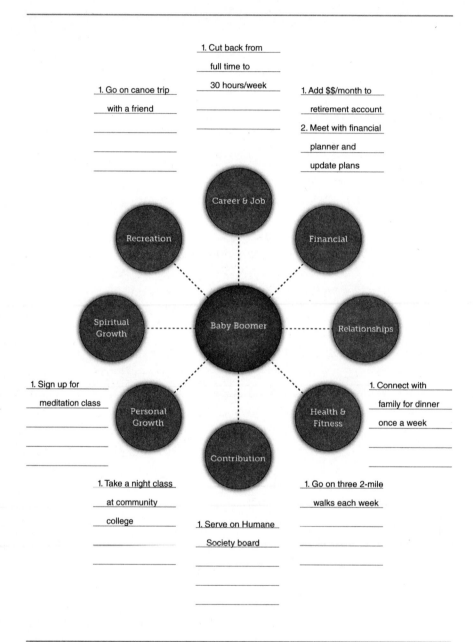

1. Sign up for
meditation class

1. Connect with
family for dinner
once a week

1. Take a night class
at community
college

1. Serve on Humane
Society board

1. Go on three 2-mile
walks each week

FIGURE 2.5   Life Decision Wheels for a Baby Boomer

sandwich generation because she's taking care of aging parents while still parenting children in college. A son who dropped out of a state university is living in the basement, and an adult daughter who lives nearby needs babysitting help with her six-month-old baby.

Do any of these scenarios resonate with you? Do some story lines? The purpose of the Life Decision Wheels is to give you *clarity* and *awareness* in areas of your life and guide you to take action steps that keep the plates spinning smoothly.

For me, the Life Decision Wheels helped compartmentalize areas in my life and have given me great awareness about what I need to be doing to stay balanced.

ANOTHER WAY TO LOOK AT LIFE BALANCE

For most, the concept of balancing life and work is nothing short of impossible. Sure, it'd be great to have everything picture-perfect, but life doesn't fit into a neat box. There are a couple schools of thought on balance, and one of those belongs to Mark C. Thompson, coauthor of *Success Built to Last*.

Thompson is famous for declaring that "Balance is BS." He argues that if you look at really driven, highly successful people, such as Bill Gates and the late Steve Jobs, there were times in their lives when they were out of balance.

When Gates was building Microsoft in the 1980s, I doubt he said, "I have to start a global campaign to eradicate smallpox and reduce deaths from measles. Then I'll have a balanced life."

Gates had other priorities, and one was creating a computer operating system that would fundamentally change the way the world did business. Sure, he probably had some sort of social life, but that was put on hold until 1994, when he was 39 years old and married Melinda French. Over the next eight years, three children came their way.

Today, if you look at Gates, he is a part-timer at Microsoft and works full-time at the Bill & Melinda Gates Foundation, where he devotes his energies to a variety of initiatives, including a goal to eliminate vaccine-preventable diseases worldwide. He is working to ensure that existing lifesaving vaccines are introduced into countries where people need them the most.

Bill Gates didn't always have a balanced life. He had highly intense periods when he was super-focused on growing his business that later gave way to periods when he was able to focus on various other aspects of life. Whether you need fulfillment or seek balance in your life, the Life Decision Wheels will help you focus on all the areas as well as make goals and action steps so that you can move the needle on a consistent basis.

BALANCE OR FULFILLMENT AND SATISFACTION

Speaker Matthew Kelly, author of *Off Balance: Getting Beyond the Work-Life Balance Myth to Personal and Professional Satisfaction*, says that instead of seeking *work-life balance*, we should focus more on achieving *work-life effectiveness*.

The fact is that work is a necessary part of life, and what happens at home (a stressful pregnancy, a sick child, a tempestuous marriage, or a death in the family) affects our work, and what happens at work (the threat of layoff, plant closure, or business failure) affects us at home.

That's why, when you create your Life Decision Wheels, your responses should accurately and honestly reflect your feelings. Where do you think you are in terms of fulfillment and satisfaction in your life? Are you finding happiness and taking pride in what you are accomplishing? Have you found the sweet spot where you are being your best in all areas of life? What steps do you need to take in each area of your life to create greater balance, satisfaction, and fulfillment?

The Life Decision Wheels guide you to a greater awareness of the different aspects of your life and of how to manage them best. Thompson's philosophy should help you realize that during different periods in life, you will be more balanced in some than in others. Following your passions and finding satisfaction and fulfillment could be even more important than balance, leading you to even greater work-life effectiveness.

The Life Decision Wheels can be beneficial in helping you get clear on where you are at this moment and where you want to be. The main idea is that you need to become aware of where you are in terms of balance, fulfillment, and satisfaction.

As you complete this chapter's exercises, you'll gain a greater awareness of what matters most in your life. This knowledge will enable you to begin making better decisions that will move you closer, step by step, to greater clarity in all areas of your life.

Joe's Recap

Life Balance and the Life Decision Wheels

- If you're busy with your career, an active social life, spending time with your family, and staying healthy by exercising, then balancing work and life may be a significant issue for you.
- It's perfectly okay to have many plates spinning at once, especially at different times in your life. The goal is to be aware of the different plates and keep them all spinning smoothly.
- Filling out the Life Decision Wheels exercise can be the key to great clarity and productivity because as you

(continued)

(continued)

segment the different areas of your life, you get more clarity on how to approach each day in an organized and focused manner.

Exercises

1. Consider the scale that follows, and then determine the number that corresponds to where you think you are in terms of life balance:

1 (Out of whack)   5 (So-so)   10 (In great balance)

_____

_____

_____

2. Where do you think you are in terms of satisfaction for your life?

1 (No satisfaction) 5 (Down the middle) 10 (Happy days are here)

_____

_____

_____

3. Some might say they're not balanced but they're fulfilled. Some might say they're balanced but not fulfilled. Some might say they're not balanced or fulfilled. What are your numbers telling you? What do you have to do to move your numbers toward a 10?_____

_____

_____

_____

4. Fill out your own Life Decision Wheels chart and start to create more balance in the following eight areas that will help you become more effective in your professional and personal life. What specific plans do you need to make in each area to be sure you are touching each plate on a weekly basis?

   1. Career

   2. Financial

   3. Relationships

   4. Health and fitness

   5. Contribution

   6. Personal growth

   7. Spiritual growth

   8. Recreation

5. Once you study the Life Decision Wheels chart and reflect on your life, list five steps you can take to move toward greater balance and fulfillment in your life.

   1.

   2.

   3.

   4.

   5.

(continued)

(continued)

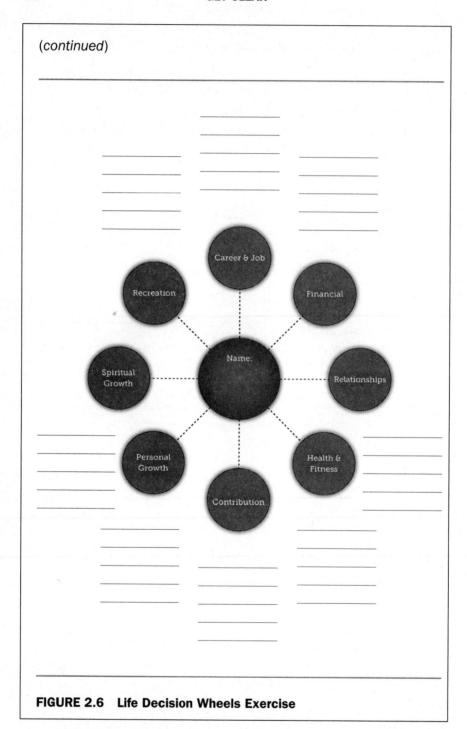

FIGURE 2.6   Life Decision Wheels Exercise

CHAPTER 3

Get Clear with Your Life Mission

Get Clear

Life moves pretty fast. If you don't stop and look around once in a while, you could miss it.

—Matthew Broderick, from the movie
Ferris Bueller's Day Off

Of all the talks I've given since publishing *Networking Is a Contact Sport,* more than two dozen have been on university campuses. The more I talk to students, the more I hear anxiety in their voices. Often, they can see the finish line of graduation, but they can't see beyond the tape. In challenging economic times, they fear having to take a job they won't like—or not finding a job at all.

I tapped into their pain and anxiety when I gave the commencement speech at Cardinal Stritch University, a four-year Franciscan university in my hometown of Fox Point, 10 miles north of Milwaukee.

I gripped the podium and looked out at a sea of black-clad graduates with their mortarboards, sitting politely inside the Wisconsin Center in downtown Milwaukee. About 1,000 students were graduating, and several thousand family members were in attendance that Sunday afternoon in the middle of May.

"So, what are you going to be when you grow up?" I asked.

I observed the knowing looks that the fresh-faced students shot each other. I cleared my throat and continued.

"You have probably been asked what you want to be when you grow up a thousand times. When you were younger, your answer might have been, 'I want to be an astronaut' or 'a firefighter,' or 'the president of the United States.'

Then you got to high school, and everyone asked you, 'Where are you going to college?' And then you came to Cardinal Stritch and the question from adults changed again. This time it was 'What are you majoring in?' You probably hated being asked that, too. And now, even though you are graduating from college, the questions haven't stopped, even though you're grown up and have decided on a major. What people really want to know is, 'Where are you headed in life?'"

I paused before continuing. I figured that a college graduation ceremony was not the time or place to shine a light on the fact that someone—a parent, the student, the state, or a government loan—had paid between $80,000 and $200,000 for the piece of parchment they were about to be handed by either the college president or the dean of students.

I smiled and said, "Since the majority of college students have no idea what they are going to do when they graduate, you can relax. You're in good company."

I assured the audience that even the most established and certain people are still curious about where they are headed in life. I went on to explain that some of the most successful people in history were also unsure of where they were going.

I can't remember what I told my parents' friends regarding my plans after I graduated from college. I would have never predicted that I'd go on to graduate school and become a business owner, an entrepreneur, a private equity investor, and most recently, an author and speaker. Most important, I learned that *life is more than work*.

Actually, I knew what I wanted to be back in my early twenties. Here's what I wanted to be:

- A good son to my parents and a good brother to my nine siblings
- A good husband
- A good father
- A loyal and supportive friend who gives back to his community
- Someone unafraid to show his passions, weaknesses, and vulnerabilities to others
- A guy who helps others by coaching and mentoring
- Someone who believes that life is a place we go to give, not get

After presenting that list to the Cardinal Stritch graduating class, I returned to my opening statement. "So when someone asks you the question, 'What do you want to be when you grow up?' these kinds of answers are much more important than saying that you want to become an engineer, a business owner, or a lawyer … important as those may be. You see, the relationships we build, the commitments we make, and the values we live by—these are the things that determine what kind of people we are. If you don't do a good job of determining what type of person you are, it won't matter *what* kind of job you have," I emphasized.

> **Worth Repeating**
>
> The relationships we build, the commitments we make, the values we live by—these are the things that determine what kind of people we are. If you don't do a good job of determining what type of person you are, it won't matter *what* kind of job you have.
>
> —Joe Sweeney

"So, instead of worrying about what you're going to be now, the focus should be on this: What is your life mission going to be? What is it that you are called to do? What do you think you're destined to become? When you answer those questions, then you'll be come exactly what you've always wanted to be."

A WINNING FORMULA

Afterward, I had several graduates approach me and say basically the same thing: "Mr. Sweeney, that's kind of a big question—what's my life mission? I just need a job!"

I've spoken with hundreds of students the past few years, and from our conversations, I can tell that the anxiety and stress levels are off the charts.

You may think you need a job but what you really need to discover first is your life mission. Even though this is a lifelong process of discovery, the following formula will help you get started on the path no matter what phase of life you are in:

passions + strengths + service to others = life mission

In other words, if you take your passions and add them to your strengths and your service to others, then you will be on the path to discovering your mission in life.

I've prepared a set of exercises at the end of this chapter where you can list what your passions and greatest strengths are, which will help show you how you can combine your attributes and characteristics to find your purpose and life mission. These will be some of the most important exercises you'll do in this book, so be sure to spend some time on them. Now let's break down what I mean by passions, strengths, and service to others.

Passions

What are you passionate about? What are you enthusiastic about? What do you delight in doing, love pursuing, or dream about doing? What interests you or is a pastime of yours? What are you absolutely obsessed about?

In the area of passions at the end of this chapter, list the things you do where you lose track of time—or wish you could hold back the clock hands because you're enjoying what you're doing so much. These are jobs that you would do for no money, as long as you could survive.

Janet Bray Attwood and Chris Attwood, coauthors of *The Passion Test: The Effortless Path to Discovering Your Life Purpose*, believe you can identify the activities that you love to do more than anything else. They say that if you write down your top five passions, you can prioritize your goals, wants, and desires in a way that helps you identify your core passions. The Passion Test is a great tool.

Janet Bray Attwood gets it when it comes to having clarity about your passions. "When I'm clear, what I want will show up in my life, and only to the extent I'm clear," she says.

But I don't know what I am passionate about. When you are passionate about something, you don't notice what time it is because you're so engrossed in what you are doing. Passions are tasks that when you're done, you say, *I can't believe how much fun that was!* That is when you know you're following your passions.

Strengths

Your strengths are the skills you possess that you are best at and have worked hard to develop. Strengths can be acquired from education and experience. For instance, you may have computer skills or speak another language, such as Spanish or Cantonese. Perhaps you have a master of business administration degree or certain job training that gives you a leg up on the competition.

You better know what your true strengths are and continuously nurture and develop them. You must also be prepared to talk about your strengths in a way that helps you stand out from the crowd. Unfortunately, many people fail to recognize their talents because (1) they've never gotten quiet and reflected about them, or (2) they never did an honest science-based assessment of their skills.

There are all sorts of tests and models you can take to identify your strengths, but if you were to ask your parents, your relatives, your friends, your colleagues, or your roommates, "What do you think I'm good at?" you'd likely get some good answers. Keep in mind, though, that many people will tell you what you're good at, but will be reluctant to discuss what you're bad at.

If you're looking for a solid, science-based resource on discovering your strengths, *StrengthsFinder 2.0* by Tom Rath can help you identify your key talents and patterns of thoughts, feelings, and behaviors that influence you. Rath makes the point that your unique and innate talents, when multiplied by the investment of time spent practicing, developing skills, and building knowledge, become your strengths. No amount of training, he says, will help you excel in your areas of weakness, meaning you can't be anything you want to be because you're not going to be good at everything. But you can work with your talents and become extraordinarily skilled.

Follow Your Bliss

Identifying and focusing on a life mission is a key step to getting clear. Joseph Campbell, who lived from 1904 to 1987, was known as an American mythologist for his work with Native Americans as well as for his study of comparative mythology and comparative religion; his philosophy can be summarized by his catchphrase: "Follow your bliss."

This doesn't mean you only do what feels good now. Campbell encouraged people to transform their lives by getting quiet and looking inside. He believed that if you followed your passions, invisible hands would guide you. Furthermore, he stated that highly clear and focused people were confident that the future would be bigger and better than the past and that they could make a positive difference.

In his book *Hero with a Thousand Faces*, Campbell presented something he called the *cosmogonic cycle*, which he defined as the eight stages that mankind goes through at one time or another. George Lucas, the creator of the *Star Wars* movies, fell in love with Campbell's philosophies and acknowledged that his writings inspired the religious and mythical themes in the *Star Wars* films. In fact, Lucas befriended Campbell and asked the author to come live at his Skywalker Ranch in northern California's Marin County. Campbell said yes and lived the last four years of his life on the ranch.

Service to Others

When most think of service, they may think of Mother Teresa serving the poor or being involved with a local soup kitchen for the homeless. With the exception of military service and risking one's life to protect our freedoms, I believe the number one service a person can provide is to start or build a business and provide a living for 10, 20, 50, or more families.

Serving others was the central message of my first book, *Networking Is a Contact Sport*. Actively pursuing opportunities to serve others helps the journey of others go more smoothly, but the real result of adopting a mind-set of serving reverberates far beyond that. As you make helping others a main objective, you will establish a reputation in your industry for being thoughtful and generous. These small gestures will foster and build around you a network of like-minded people with relationships that will open up new and different opportunities.

As for the places where you can be of service, the possibilities are all around you:

- You can serve others where you work.
- You can serve others where you live.
- You can serve others where you exercise or play a sport.
- You can serve others where you socialize.

- You can serve others where you go to church, if you belong to a faith community.

You'll understand why it's better to give than to receive when you reach out and ask what you can do for others. Life is not about transactional relationships. People tire of others who are looking for a quid pro quo, so you'll never build any sort of deep relationship because these relationships are based on what others can do for you.

Instead, look for opportunities to step up and offer to assist without first analyzing what the benefit is for you.

So, what are you passionate about? What are your strengths? Are you actively working toward serving others? If you're still unsure how to answer any of these questions, know that you are not alone. You are taking steps in the right direction.

Early Adopter

Like the Cardinal Stitch graduates, most young people don't discover their passion or their life mission until after college, but there are many who do.

In my family, that would be our son Conor, the second of four children. Even at nine years of age, he was interested in politics. He would beg us to stay up and watch the election results on TV. It didn't matter if it was a presidential election or an off-year election; Conor loved the whole political process. Whereas I'd nod off to sleep by 10 PM, Conor had no problem staying awake until midnight or beyond until the election results were in.

During his junior year of college, Conor participated in Marquette University's Les Aspin Center for Government program in Washington, DC, where he interned with Representative Paul Ryan in 2007. Conor was thinking of going to law school, but Representative Ryan asked him to stay on as a legislative aide. A year later after college, Representative Ryan asked Conor—just 23 years old—to be his press secretary, a big honor at such a young age.

Conor followed his passion from a young age. If there's something you've always wanted to do, follow your passion and listen to the voice inside; you're never too old to do something you've always wanted to do.

Maybe you felt you had a life mission at one time, but something got in the way. Many of us encounter detours along the way that often help us develop other skills or provide new or otherwise unavailable opportunities. The important question today is: Where are you going now? The following questions will help to give you clarity.

THE BIG EIGHT QUESTIONS

So, what if you aren't sure what your life mission is? The following set of questions, the Big Eight, will help you think more critically about what truly matters to you and identify what your life mission is.

1. Why Are You Here?

Have you ever thought about why you were put on this earth? This is a huge philosophical question and can be answered in many different ways. But identifying what you wish to achieve during your lifetime and establishing a plan to get there will give you more focus, more drive, and a greater sense of self-assurance than if you haven't yet defined what your plan is. Knowing why you're here or believing you're on this earth for a reason will help you get clear and give you confidence that you're on the right path in life.

2. Who Do You Want to Be When You Grow Up?

This question is different from "What do you want to do when you grow up?" Who you are is more important than what you do. The strength of your character and the choices you make about who you want to be have a greater impact on your life than any decisions you make or goals you achieve from nine to five, Monday through Friday.

So what type of person do you want to be? How do you want people around you to describe you? Trustworthy? Honest? Hard-working?

3. What Is Your Life Mission?

Have you given thought to what your true life mission is? I truly believe my life mission is to help others by making their lives easier or helping them discover who they truly want to be. So what is your life mission? What are the things you wish you had more time to do? When you look back on your life, what are the things you want to be able to say you accomplished? What are the things you fear you will most regret not doing if you don't get around to doing them?

4. Do You Take Full Responsibility for What Happens in Your Life?

Life is filled with challenges. If you can maintain focus and continue to forge ahead despite setbacks, distractions, and adversity, you will be better positioned to come out the other side stronger, wiser, and more experienced.

Whatever life throws at you—and life has a way of throwing curveballs—you are still 100 percent responsible for how you react to what happens in your life. No matter how great the obstacles, circumstances, or uncertainties you face, the choices you make, your commitment to your goals, and your ability to overcome obstacles determine your success.

5. How Do You Differentiate Yourself from Others?

This one is easier than you think. If you focus on giving and serving, others around you will notice that you are different from those with a me-first, self-centered attitude. Also, if you develop a habit of continuous learning and improvement, you will quickly develop a reputation for being the person that people know to go to for sound advice, reliable information, and good counsel.

6. How Can You Do a Better Job of Building and Serving the Community You Are a Part Of?

You build your community by actively and consistently engaging with others through both traditional channels and social media. Whatever the channel of communication—whether an unscheduled sales call or a scheduled tweet—every interaction is an opportunity to grow a community around you. The more accessible, helpful, and positive you are in your interactions, the more your community will grow. Building a community of friends, fans, and business associates will take time but is directly related to the effort you put into establishing a community.

Your Community Is Everything

Do you have a community?

If you are like most, your community is a bit disjointed, looks different depending on how people engage with you, and would benefit from a little more attention from you. You are likely already a part of many communities online and off. Are you connecting with these individuals and inviting them to connect with you and with others in your network?

If not, the answer may be penning a blog for the niche industry you're a part of to foster an exchange of

(continued)

(continued)

knowledge. It could be organizing meetings, community events, or an online forum for local businesses in your town to share ideas. Establishing a community requires you to be a problem solver, thought leader, and agent of change.

Community building happens online a lot today. If you have a website, make it easy to navigate and be consistent. Have a loyalty or referral program so that your customers feel rewarded or are incentivized. Don't forget that your online communication, whether through a blog, Facebook, Twitter, or traditional e-mail, is your responsibility. Dedicate time to advancing your industry or community by sharing information that benefits the reader. The result is that you establish a reputation as a thought leader in this space while growing your community.

Here are some other ideas to work with:

- On the personal side, reach out to *family, friends, and neighbors* through phone calls and social gatherings.
- On the professional side, engage with *coworkers, supervisors, and corporate executives* whom you might know.
- In the area of associations, be part of *alumni, education, and professional or trade associations*.
- Locally, take time to build relationships with *owners of dry cleaners, clothing stores, hair salons, and other small businesses*.
- Build a network of professionals—*physicians, lawyers, accountants, and bankers*—you might know.
- In the faith community, look toward your *church or support groups*.
- In the local community, connect with *service organizations, volunteer groups, sports organizations, and kids' sports associations*.

7. Will You Take Action to Make Any Necessary Changes?

Change can be challenging as well. Going after what we want not only requires figuring out what that is, but also calls for overcoming many obstacles, juggling many obligations, and disproving many assumptions we have about ourselves. So, what will it take for you to step up and take action?

8. Are You Ready to Make Mistakes?

Mark Twain once said, "Good decisions come from experience. Experience comes from making bad decisions." In other words, if you've made mistakes in the past, let them go. If a fear of making mistakes is holding you back, you must recognize that failure is a vital part of success and that making mistakes is better than not taking chances at all.

GETTING THERE?

Being thoughtful about the answers to questions such as these is part of getting quiet and developing a better understanding of yourself.

Joe's Recap

Get Clear with Your Life Mission

- Even more important than determining what you want to do with your life are the relationships you build, the commitments you make, and the values you live by—these are the things that define the type of person you are.
- If you know the type of person you want to be, it won't matter what type of job you have. Rather than worry about what you're going to do now, your focus should be this: *What is my life mission?* When you can answer that

(continued)

(continued)

question, it will be easier to see the steps necessary to get there.

- The questions in the exercise section below will help you determine what your passions are and what strengths you possess to help you find your purpose and mission in life. These will be some of the most important exercises you'll do in this book, so be sure to spend some time on them.

Exercises

1. Using Figure 3.1 as a guide, complete the formula of *passions + strengths + service to others = life mission* by listing three strengths of yours. (Examples: strong leadership skills, able to organize and coordinate many details, active in a large community, or great interpersonal skills.)
   1.
   2.
   3.
2. List three passions of yours. (Examples: to help others do things they never thought they could do, speaking and teaching, or participating in outdoor activities and exercise.)
   1.
   2.
   3.
3. List three ways to serve others. (Examples: mentoring, teaching, making connections, or sharing information.)
   1.
   2.
   3.

4. Construct a life mission statement that combines your skills and passions with the goals you want to achieve. (Example: I want to use my leadership skills and connections [strengths] to help others become the best version of themselves [passion] by teaching and mentoring in the areas of leadership, business, and career development [service to others].) There may not be a clear connection between your passions, your skills, and the service you can do for others, but often the connections forged in those unlikely places are the most rewarding and beneficial.

_____

_____

_____

5. Do you have clarity on what your life mission is? How has your life mission changed over time?

_____

_____

_____

6. What are some of the best life experiences you've had? How did they help define or change your goals?

_____

_____

_____

7. What can you do to combine your strengths, your passions, and your service to others to find your purpose and mission in life? Where do your strengths, passions, and service overlap?

_____

_____

_____

(*continued*)

(*continued*)

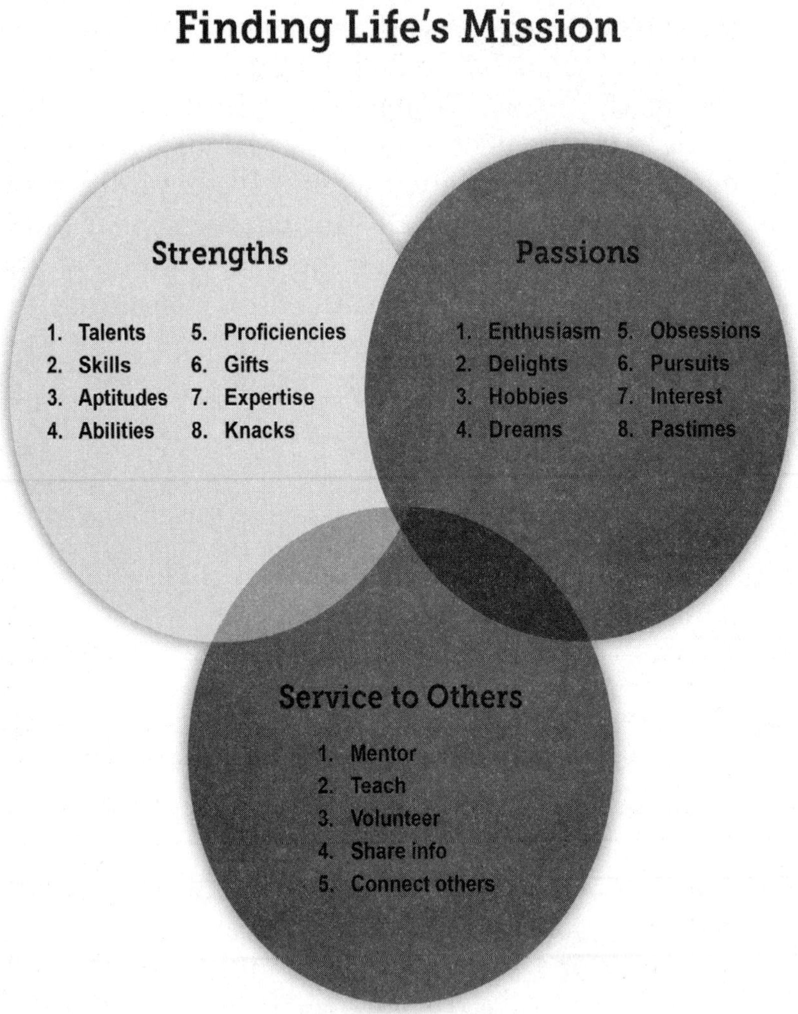

Finding Life's Mission

Strengths

1. Talents   5. Proficiencies
2. Skills   6. Gifts
3. Aptitudes   7. Expertise
4. Abilities   8. Knacks

Passions

1. Enthusiasm   5. Obsessions
2. Delights   6. Pursuits
3. Hobbies   7. Interest
4. Dreams   8. Pastimes

Service to Others

1. Mentor
2. Teach
3. Volunteer
4. Share info
5. Connect others

FIGURE 3.1   Finding Life's Mission

CHAPTER **4**

Understanding People's Needs

Get Clear

Rules for Happiness: something to do, someone to love, something to hope for.

—IMMANUEL KANT, eighteenth-century philosopher

Developing a better understanding of the needs of others can also help you develop a better understanding of yourself.

When you're trying to get clear, you have to do more than get quiet and seek out a period of reflection, create balance, and discover your life mission. An additional step to getting clear is focusing on the needs of others and responding accordingly. When you tune in to other people's needs, you become less focused on yourself. Taking the needs of others into consideration adds clarity and perspective to our decisions.

When it comes to the basic needs in life, three yearnings stand out above the rest:

- The need to belong to something greater than oneself.
- The need to love and be loved.
- The need to know that your life has meaning and that you made a difference to others.

Let's take a closer look at each of these three needs.

THE NEED TO BELONG

The greatest companies in the world have achieved dominance by figuring out the needs of their customers and fulfilling those needs.

Harley-Davidson motorcycle riders are mighty proud of their Harleys, but what most people don't know is that Harley-Davidson was headed to oblivion in the 1970s and early 1980s when Japanese manufacturers flooded the market with high-quality, low-cost bikes. Unable to compete on price, Harley-Davidson had to find a new path to profitability and relevance. The company chose to focus on the emotional connection—the feelings of personal freedom and independence that people enjoyed with their Harley-Davidsons—through its advertising and marketing campaigns. "Harley-Davidson motorcycles represent the adventurous pioneer spirit, the Wild West, having your own horse and going where you want to go," said its president and chief executive officer, Richard Teerlink.

Of course, selling the joy of riding the open road didn't solve its problems. The legendary company had to put some traction to its new mission, and it did that by establishing and fostering lifelong relationships between the Harley-Davidson brand and its customers. The result was the formation of the Harley Owners Group, or H.O.G.

H.O.G. helped establish a bond between the brand and the customer by creating communities of loyal customers and evangelists. The formation of H.O.G. chapters in small towns, large cities, and around the world turned around flagging sales and made Harley-Davidson profitable again. These days, H.O.G. is the world's largest factory-sponsored motorcycle club, with more than 1 million members and 1,400 official chapters.

What Harley-Davidson did was tap into the fundamental need we all have to belong to something bigger than ourselves. When you buy a Harley-Davidson motorcycle, you become part of a family. If you've ever been to a H.O.G. rally, where Harley-Davidson riders arrive with a roar and everyone hangs out in their leathers, then you know what I'm talking about. It's all about having a passion for something and sharing that passion with others. The team at Harley-Davidson understood that everyone wants to belong to something bigger than themselves. They understood *the value of giving customers a sense of belonging*.

Now compare what Harley-Davidson did to another iconic brand—BMW, as represented by the logos for Harley-Davidson and for BMW.

Nearly everyone on the planet recognizes the circular blue-and-white BMW logo or roundel found on BMW sedans, SUVs, and motorcycles—or *Motorräder*, as they're called in Germany, their country of origin.

BMW motorcycles are considered the best and most elegant in the world. When the Michigan State Police were looking to replace its aging Harleys recently, it conducted performance tests between new Harley-Davidson models and BMW motorcycles. The results weren't even close: BMWs were faster, handled better, and were safer than Harleys by a wide margin.

Anecdotes like this are common, so why are Harley-Davidsons more popular than BMW motorcycles, even though by every measure BMW bikes are better machines? Because Harley-Davidson has successfully tapped into the fundamental human need to belong to something greater than yourself when you purchase a Fat Boy or a Forty-Eight ride.

THE NEED FOR LOVE

Another of the strongest human needs is to love and be loved. One company that has long understood *the need for love* is Coca-Cola. Its famous Hilltop advertising campaign in the 1970s featured 65 young people from a variety of nations, in clothing representing their nationalities, standing on a dewy hillside, holding bottles of Coca-Cola and singing a catchy jingle about buying the world a Coke and teaching the world to sing in perfect harmony.

The "I'd Like to Teach the World to Sing" campaign resonated with people everywhere. People felt good about others—and themselves—when they sang along. Suddenly buying a Coke took on a much greater meaning. The focus of the message wasn't the product; it was openness, generosity, and change. The ad became so popular that it prompted the release of a full-length version of the song, with a portion of the proceeds being donated to United Nations Children's Fund (UNICEF).

> ### The Need to Love and Be Loved
>
> People will forget what you said, people will forget what you did, but people will never forget how you made them feel.
>
> —Maya Angelou, poet

As the poet Maya Angelou once said, "People will forget what you said, people will forget what you did, but people will never forget how you made them feel." That idea underscores why Coca-Cola has been one of the top consumer brands for the past 80 years.

Understanding the universal need to love and be loved and understanding how your words or actions can make people feel is a very important part of connecting with people.

TAKING CARE OF THOSE CLOSEST TO YOU

I'm a perpetual optimist who believes life has great meaning and can be used to make a great difference in people's lives. Being able to protect, provide for, and create a sense of security for the ones you love are innate desires. Life insurance agents and financial services executives remind you that you don't buy life insurance for yourself but for your spouse and children.

There are companies whose corporate cultures are based on understanding the needs of their customers and the importance of connecting with them. Do you practice this with your coworkers, business acquaintances, and friends?

Let me share a story of how I try to connect with people. Nearly every morning, I drop by Sendik's Food Market in my hometown of Fox Point on my way to downtown Milwaukee. Sendik's is one of those local grocery stores where customers and employees are on a first-name basis.

When I walk up to the counter with my morning coffee, I nod to Kenny, the Sendik's clerk whom I call Special K. He knows that I'm going to hand him a $5 bill for a $1.25 cup of coffee. He knows not to give me any change. The extra goes toward buying the coffee and a morning treat for the person behind me.

On one occasion, as I headed out of Sendik's, the patron behind me stopped me.

"Hey, thanks for the cup of coffee," he said and grinned. "That's pretty cool. I really appreciate it."

"No problem."

"Why did you do it?"

"I want to make someone's day a little brighter. I like catching their looks of surprise. Some cry; some buy coffee for the person behind them."

"That's great. You ought to write a book about that."

"Actually, I just did." Two months earlier, *Networking Is a Contact Sport* had been released, and I had mentioned how I bought coffee for folks waiting in line at Sendik's.

The cheery man stuck out his hand. "Hi, I'm Ed Zore."

"Joe Sweeney. Hey, I know you. Aren't you the chairman of the board of Northwestern Mutual?"

"Yes, I am. Listen, I'd love to read your book."

"I'll have one sent over to your office."

When I got to my office, I signed a book and had it delivered to Northwestern Mutual's corporate offices just a couple of blocks away. Two weeks later, I received a handwritten, heartfelt note from Ed saying thanks for the coffee and that he loved the book, loved my networking philosophy, and would love to find out how to get his 9,000 agents to network like me.

Within a few months, I'd spoken at the Northwestern Mutual Lives Leaders Summit and the Northwestern Mutual Financial Planning Conference, and I'd conducted workshops and keynotes for Northwestern Mutual.

The moral of the story is that I didn't buy Ed a cup of coffee so that I could get something in return. What I've learned over the years is that random acts of kindness can come back 100-fold. We often get so busy in life that we forget about doing out-of-the-ordinary gestures for others. Simple acts of kindness never go out of style.

We can't afford to be so busy that we don't understand the universal need to belong to something greater than ourselves, to love and be loved, and to make a difference to those around us. Somehow, taking the focus off yourself and the issues you're dealing with frees you up to tune in to the lives of others and help them meet their basic needs of belonging, loving, and making a difference.

You'll be amazed how looking outward instead of inward adds clarity and vision to who you want to be and what you want to do with your life.

Joe's Recap

You Can Get Clear When You Understand People's Needs

- Three basic needs in life stand out above the rest: the need to belong, the need to love and be loved, and the need to know that your life has meaning and you made a difference to others.
- The Harley-Davidson brand recognizes the need people have to belong. The formation of the Harley Owners Group, or H.O.G., which has become the world's largest factory-sponsored motorcycle club, tapped into the idea of personal freedom.
- Harley-Davidson understood the fundamental need we all have to belong to something bigger than ourselves. When you buy a Harley-Davidson motorcycle, you become part of a family.
- Coca-Cola showed that the soft drink company understood the need to love by creating "I Want to Teach the World to Sing (in Perfect Harmony)" television advertisements in the 1970s.
- Companies such as Harley-Davidson and Coca-Cola understand that people will forget what you said, that people will forget what you did, but that people will never forget how you made them feel, according to poet Maya Angelou.
- You'll be surprised how doing something for others when they don't expect it takes the focus off yourself and frees you up to tune in to the lives of others.

Exercise

1. How can understanding these three needs help with your business, your clients, and your life (Figure 4.1)?
(continued)

(continued)

Basic Needs	
Needs	What can you do to meet these three needs of your clients, coworkers, friends, and future employers?
Belonging	1. 2. 3.
Love and Be Loved	1. 2. 3.
Make a Difference and Have Meaning in Life	1. 2. 3.

FIGURE 4.1   Meeting Three Basic Needs

CHAPTER 5

Clarity in Differentiating Yourself

Get Clear

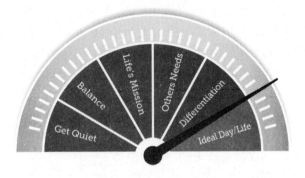

In the end, all business operations can be reduced to three words: people, product, and profits.

—LEE IACOCCA, former CEO and chairman of Chrysler and credited with inventing the minivan, the precursor to the SUV

Having clarity means having a strong sense of self, which is vital for differentiating yourself from others. When you view yourself as highly desirable (because of your work skills), uniquely obtainable (because you're confident you can do the job), and economically irresistible (because you add value to a company), you've taken a big step toward getting clear.

In a similar fashion, the world's best companies understand this concept when producing products or services that are highly desirable, uniquely obtainable, and economically irresistible. Not many achieve this lofty status, but one that stands out is Apple, one of the biggest companies in the world behind giants such as Walmart and ExxonMobil.

So the question is this: How did Apple get clear and come to market with so many great tech products? How did it become highly desirable, uniquely obtainable, and economically irresistible? The answer is it got close to its customers, which was founder Steve Jobs's idea all along. He and Apple figured out not only what people want, but also what their needs would be in the future.

Getting close to the customer has been Apple's core mission since 1976, when Jobs and Steve Wozniak started tinkering in the garage of Jobs's family home in Los Altos, California. Their goal was to put a personal computer in the hands of everyday people, and you could say that they succeeded beyond their wildest dreams.

Back in the 1970s and early 1980s, the idea of a personal computer was *Popular Science* stuff and the province of nerds. Only techies were qualified to turn on the early Atari or Wang computers that were often sold in kit form. Jobs got it when it came to inventing a new way of computing that would be highly desirable to consumers. He made sure the headline of Apple's first marketing brochure in 1977 proclaimed this tagline: "Simplicity is the ultimate sophistication."

Jobs believed that a core component of design simplicity was making products that were intuitively easy to use. "Plug and play" was the catchphrase, which was simple to say but hard to execute. A breakthrough occurred when Jobs used the metaphor of viewing the computer screen like a desktop.

The Apple founder understood that the number one fear people had about technology was *technology*. Jobs comprehended that most users weren't 16-year-old kids who adapted quickly to technological advances, but were average folks from a variety of backgrounds who didn't have time to thumb through a manual and figure out a bunch of instructions to get their devices going. Jobs and Apple made it easy.

The other large company that did a really good job of creating a product that was highly desirable, uniquely attainable, and economically irresistible was Chrysler with the introduction of the minivan in the 1980s.

Before then, young families got around in cramped station wagons with low ceilings or box-shaped vehicles, such as the flat-nosed Volkswagen van, which topped out at 35 miles per hour on any sort of incline. In the early 1980s, Chrysler CEO and chair Lee Iacocca, a lifelong car guy, saw an opportunity to produce a larger car that could haul kids and have plenty of room for school backpacks and groceries. He brought in domestic engineers—the soccer moms of America—for a series of focus groups.

Questions were asked:

- "How many seats would be ideal?"
- "How important is head room for you and your children?"
- "How do you load groceries in the car?"
- "How much room do you need for trips to the home improvement store?"
- "Do your kids eat meals in the car?"
- "If you could have cup holders, where should they be and how big?"

Remember, the early 1980s was when a huge swath of baby boomers were having children, so there was a growing need for a kid hauler. As any new parent will tell you, once you have children, your car needs change.

What young parents wanted was a family room on wheels—places for cups and drinks, overhead lights, comfortable seating for everyone, a feeling of roominess, and a feature that would become feasible years later, a rear-seat video entertainment system with screens in the seat backs. This made the Dodge minivan highly desirable in suburbia.

Iacocca and his design team took action and designed a new automobile segment that took the industry by storm. The first Dodge Caravans and Plymouth Voyagers rolled off the assembly lines in 1984, and the Sweeney family—with four children born between 1983 and 1989—was among the early customers. During our 33 years of marriage, I figure that outside of our home mortgage and our kids' college bills, our number three household expense was the purchase of *five* Chrysler minivans. We bought the minivans because they were easily attainable, and they were priced in an affordable way—low monthly payments—that made them economically irresistible.

Here is the key about getting clear: Iacocca and Jobs were innovators who understood that they were able to differentiate themselves in the marketplace by producing products that provided solutions and simplicity to consumers.

Jobs and Iacocca were brilliant in differentiating themselves and their companies from the competition. We can learn from these two icons about differentiating ourselves and getting close to our customers and clients.

THE FOUR-STEP PROCESS TO DIFFERENTIATING YOURSELF

You can differentiate yourself to get close to your customers and clients by using the following four-step process.

The process appears to be simple, but as with many things in life, the simplest things are often the most difficult things.

Don't let that slow you down. Instead, embrace this exercise and do your best to look for opportunities to employ them whenever you can.

The four steps are:

1. Ask.
2. Listen actively.
3. Take action.
4. Believe and receive.

When it comes to *asking*, asking politely, persistently, and creatively will give you the best chance to receive a yes or an affirmative reply.

There's another skill to asking, and that's having the ability to frame good questions. Because relationships deepen through social interaction, the ability to make interesting and thought-provoking inquiries can help you become an excellent conversationalist.

When you're in a business or social situation, make part of your interaction with people beneficial by asking interesting questions of those you are acquainted with. Just as important, start conversations with people you don't know. Seek common ground, listening closely for clues that would lead to a thoughtful and deeper conversation.

When you can't think of anything, there are two surefire topics that everyone loves to talk about—themselves and their kids. If there are two topics to steer clear of, they're politics and religion. Anything work related or the reliable discussions about family, sports, and the weather, however, are safe places to start a conversation. When in a professional setting, a great icebreaker is asking, "Do you have any travel planned?" But an even better question is "What are you most excited about in your life right now?"

Listen actively when you engage in a conversation with associates, business clients, or friends. When you listen closely to their words or the clues they leave behind, it's amazing how much you can learn and how you can receive a better perception of who that person is. Staying engaged as an active listener can be difficult, especially when you are hosting many guests, but it's well worth the effort. Although being a good listener is a rare skill, when you listen well, you connect better with others while differentiating yourself.

Listening actively means you're thoughtfully paying attention to the person you're having a conversation with. Take a long moment to give your complete attention to this person and keep it away from the various tasks or distractions you're working on. When you listen closely to what's being said, you may hear an opportunity to offer help or advice, thus giving you another chance to give, not get. Listen to others, listen to the marketplace, and listen to your gut. You were given two ears and one mouth, so use them in proportion.

When you *take action*, you're showing others that you follow up on promises to do something, such as "Let me e-mail you his contact information so that you have it."

This is all too common in business, where a business associate either says he or she will get back to me or fails to respond to a call for action on an item of vital interest to both of us. It could be a sign of the times, but staying true to your word never goes out of style. Those who offer to take action and follow through are getting rarer these days, but they are still valued for following through and taking action.

Many of us ask and listen but don't take the next step because of fear. Our two greatest fears are the fear of rejection and the fear of failure.

Many who don't take action come armed with excuses. Dr. Wayne W. Dyer, author of *Excuses Begone! How to Change Lifelong, Self-Defeating Thinking Habits*, wrote the book on overcoming excuses.[1] He surveyed thousands of people and came up with 5,000 excuses that people regularly employ. Then he whittled them down to a list of 18 common excuses that stop people from accomplishing what they would like to accomplish:

1. "It will be difficult."
2. "It's going to be risky."
3. "It will take a long time."
4. "There will be family drama."
5. "I don't deserve it."
6. "It's not my nature."
7. "I can't afford it."
8. "No one will help me."
9. "It has never happened before."
10. "I'm not strong enough."
11. "I'm not smart enough."
12. "I'm too old," or "I'm too young."
13. "The rules won't let me."
14. "It's too big."
15. "I don't have the energy."

16. "It's my personal family history."
17. "I'm too busy."
18. "I'm too scared."

We've all uttered one, two, or all of these excuses at one time or another. The key point is to remind yourself that these excuses are just that—excuses—and that you have the ability to accomplish any task you set your mind to. People take notice when you take action and follow through on something you said you were going to do.

Finally, the phrase *believe and receive* refers to having faith in yourself and what you're doing. When you believe in your ability to help others, you will receive far more than you ever imagined.

These four steps are so important. When you go through the progression—ask, listen, take action, and believe and receive— you create a foundation that often leads to personal and professional success. *You* will make yourself highly desirable, uniquely obtainable, and economically irresistible—just like iPhones and minivans.

Joe's Recap

Clarity in Differentiating Yourself

- Contemplate your uniqueness and what differentiates you from others. You want to figure out how you can become more highly desirable, uniquely attainable, and economically irresistible. Understanding this is a key step in getting clear.
- If you look at business examples, not many companies or individuals have all three characteristics. Two that stand out are Apple and Chrysler. How can you differentiate yourself and your business?

(continued)

(*continued*)

- These four steps will help you see major advances in the way you can get clear, get free, and get going. They are:

  1. Ask.

  2. Listen actively.

  3. Take action.

  4. Believe and receive.

- *Ask* means to ask politely, persistently, and creatively, which will give you the best chance to receive a yes or an affirmative reply.

- *Listening actively* means you're giving someone your complete attention. When you listen closely to what's being said, you may hear an opportunity to offer help or advice, thus giving you another chance to give, not get.

- *Taking action* means that you follow up on promises to do something, whether it's running down a request or finding out information.

- Finally, *believe and receive* means having faith in yourself and what you're doing. When you really believe something is going to happen, it's remarkable how many times it really does.

Exercises

1. What's the last product you purchased that you thought was highly desirable, uniquely attainable, and economically irresistible? Did those attributes turn out to be true?

_____

_____

_____

2. How can you become more highly desirable, uniquely attainable, and economically irresistible to others?

_____

_____

_____

3. Can you think of examples when you asked creatively? Actively listened? Acted intentionally? Believed strongly in your ability to help others?

_____

_____

_____

4. Of the ask, listen, take action, and believe and receive steps, which ones are you best at? Why?

_____

_____

_____

5. Which ones could you improve on? How?

_____

_____

_____

CHAPTER 6

Getting Clear by Creating Your Ideal Day and Ideal Life

Get Clear

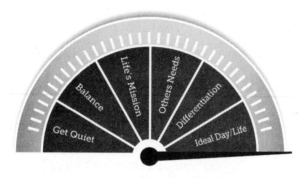

The best day of your life is the one on which you decide your life is your own. No apologies or excuses. No one to lean on, rely on, or blame. The gift is yours—it is an amazing journey—and you alone are responsible for the quality of it. This is the day your life really begins.

—BOB MOAWAD, coauthor of *The Secret of the Slight Edge: How to Get Out of Your Own Way*

Back in 2000, our family embarked on a midwinter getaway to Mexico's Playa del Carmen, located on the Yucatan peninsula 40 miles south of Cancun. It was an ideal vacation and gave me a unique opportunity to reflect on where I had been in life and where I was going.

A friend had recommended that I read a book by Bob Buford titled *Halftime: Moving from Success to Significance*. I dove into

Halftime while I relaxed on the warm sands of Playa del Carmen's tropical beach and the kids frolicked in the water.

Buford's insights struck a chord with me. From his perspective as a successful cable TV pioneer and venture philanthropist, Buford wrote that your forties and fifties—the midlife years—are a great time to pause and consider how to make the transition to living the ideal life.[1]

Buford outlined several exercises in the book, starting with examining where you think you are in life and where you want to be. I was supposed to take my time doing this—maybe a few hours. He directed me to close my eyes and let my imagination roam. "Make a picture of your life as it would be if it were perfect," Buford wrote. "Visualize where you would be, what you would be doing, and who you would be doing it with. Say, 'This is my most ideal day—the perfect day of my dreams.'"

I sat down with a pad of paper and began outlining my perfect day. I had no trouble filling up a couple of pages with the details of my ideal day. Then I chronicled what I'd do hour by hour—from the time I woke up to the time I went to bed. I wrote about having time in my day to get to the gym and swim some laps and on other days grabbing lunch with friends. I described having time to make progress on longer-term projects and finishing my workday early enough to get home and spend time with my family.

The exercise was invigorating and satisfying—until Buford confronted me with a follow-up question: "What did you do today to live your ideal day?"

Well, Buford had me there. Up until then, I had never actually thought about my ideal day. I just got up every morning and did what I had to do.

When I saw what my ideal day *could* look like, though, I realized that it was achievable but that I hadn't actually been working toward getting there. Buford made the point that if you don't think about what you want to happen in your life each day—as well as maintain a focus on what your longer-term goals are—then it likely isn't going to happen.

In actuality, having your best day, every day, is within your control, and it doesn't require much work at all. But it starts the night before with thinking through the day ahead and preparing to be your best self after a good night's sleep.

Your Ideal Day		
Time	Your Current Day	Your Ideal Day
6 a.m.		
7 a.m.		
8 a.m.		
9 a.m.		
10 a.m.		
11 a.m.		
12 p.m.		
1 p.m.		
2 p.m.		
3 p.m.		
4 p.m.		
5 p.m.		
6 p.m.		
7 p.m.		
8 p.m		
9 p.m.		
10 p.m.		

FIGURE 6.1 Your Ideal Day

The message in *Halftime* was a game changer for me, and it can be for you. If Buford's exercise can get you thinking about what you need to do to live an ideal day, then why not do the same to live an ideal week? And why stop there? What would your ideal month, ideal year, and yes, ideal life, look like? The more you're energized to fulfill your goals, the better chance you have to succeed in your life, in your work, and in your relationships.

PLANNING YOUR IDEAL WEEK

To ensure I was making progress toward achieving my ideal week, I began setting aside 20 to 30 minutes every Sunday evening to review the week ahead. I looked at upcoming meetings and noted what needed to be done so that I would be prepared for them. If the week included business trips, what needed to be packed? Were there any breakfast, lunch, or dinner meetings with clients? What about family time, kids' games and practices, and social obligations? Was I keeping all the plates spinning? Should I glance at my Life Decision Wheels again to see where I stood?

Then I looked at how my obligations coordinated with the times I wanted to work out. I also jotted down reminders to drink water because so often this very simple, but essential, detail is overlooked. I gave this part of my planning a name: *FEW* meetings, an acronym for proper *f*ood, daily *e*xercise, and adequate *w*ater.

PLANNING YOUR IDEAL MONTH

I didn't stop at trying to achieve the ideal week. I turned to monthly planning. I wrote down goals for each month and divided them into four categories (Figure 6.2):

- Business
- Personal
- Family, spirituality, and health
- Financial

Your Ideal Month	
Business	**Financial**
Personal	**Health, Spirituality, & Family**

FIGURE 6.2 Your Ideal Month

These are the same categories identified in the Winning Action Plan in Chapter 1. They are great goals to monitor every month because days and weeks flash by in a blur, and before you know it, another year rolls around.

PLANNING YOUR IDEAL YEAR

You might want to think about planning for your ideal year. You can tap notes into your iPhone or smartphone device, or you may choose to use a more low-tech planner. The key is to find and implement an organizational system that truly works for you. Although there's no reason you can't keep all this information electronically, you might find that a handwritten organizing resource works better for you.

On the day after Thanksgiving, I take time to reflect on the past year and plan for the New Year ahead. I review my calendar and photos as well as the events, projects, and people that have been a part of my life. As I take stock and map out the upcoming year, I become empowered as I see myself moving toward my ideal year. As soon as the ball drops at Time Square, I'm ready to go and can't wait for the New Year to get into full swing.

PLANNING YOUR IDEAL LIFE

Whatever resource you use to organize your life—whether a planner or a smartphone—you need to have something in your hands that helps establish a picture of where your life is headed. This takes us full circle to Buford's original directive, which was asking me to describe my ideal life and what it would look like if it really turned out great.

Of course, circumstances change and life takes unexpected turns. You can make all the plans in the world, and unforeseen situations can alter the best-laid plans. But that doesn't mean you shouldn't make plans. Planning gives you the best chance to achieve your ideal life. By mapping out your ideal day, your ideal week, your ideal month, and your ideal year, you stand a better chance of realizing those goals.

Planning an ideal life is important, but it can be difficult to think that far ahead. Most of us devote more thought to planning a vacation than we do planning our ideal lives. You'll benefit greatly if you set aside even a short time to visualize what your ideal life would look like.

Key to the process of identifying and defining your ideals is writing everything down. That's why, at the end of this chapter, I've prepared an exercise that requires you to reflect and write one full page describing what your life would be like if everything turned out great. This is an exercise that you'll want to revisit three or four times each year, not only to ensure you are getting closer to your goal, but also because plans do change. If plans change, focus and goals must also be redefined. The purpose of this reflection exercise is to provide clarity in your business life as well as your personal life.

Buford's questions about what makes an ideal life reminds me of country artist Tim McGraw's song "Live Like You Were Dying," which is about a man confronted with a cancer diagnosis. McGraw lost his father, Tug McGraw, a relief pitcher for the New York Mets and the Philadelphia Phillies, to cancer, so there's poignancy to the song because the lyrics are about a man who learns he does not have long to live. Knowing that his time is limited, he says he went skydiving, mountain climbing, rode a bull named Fumanchu, and loved deeper, spoke sweeter, and forgave grudges he'd been denying.

Maintaining focus on these key issues is essential to making better decisions, managing time more effectively, and most important, living each day, knowing that time is short. Let this thought spur you to seek out the ideal life every day.

Planning for Your Ideal Clients

In addition to planning for your ideal day and ideal life, you can also add some forethought to how you can identify ideal clients for your business. To make that happen, you have to do four things well:

1. Understand the importance of serving others in business and life.
2. Identify your ideal client or market.

3. Identify the client's needs and wants.
4. Establish strategies to fulfill those needs and wants.

I've spent a lot of time the past couple of years working with companies. When executives are asked why their companies aren't growing their business, the response is often the same: *We're having a hard time identifying our ideal client, and when we do, we're spending too much time serving our targeted client.*

Here's a conversation I had with the president of a financial services company trying to increase the firm's assets from $350 million to $500 million:

"I run a financial investment company. My ideal client is someone who makes between $250,000 and $500,000 a year. He or she has a million dollars of liquid assets to invest with me. Ideally, this client is someone between the ages of 45 and 65 years old."

"So, how many clients do you have?"

"We have 267."

"How many clients fit into that mold you just described, taking in between $250,000 and $500,000 a year with liquid assets of over a million dollars?"

"Only 16. The rest are small ones."

"How big are their investment portfolios?"

"A typical one would be a retired schoolteacher with $77,000 dollars in her IRA [Individual Retirement Arrangement]."

"How often does she call you?"

"I'd say three times a month."

"Does her financial advisor spend a lot of time speaking with her?"

"Sure. There's a lot of hand-holding."

This executive told me who his ideal client was—someone earning more than $250,000. He had described

(continued)

(continued)

his company goal—increase assets by 40 percent to $500 million. But he and his financial advising team were not living that out. How were they going to push assets north of $350 million if they were spending half their time with their smaller clients? He needed to start focusing on reaching their ideal clients if they were going to increase the firm's assets by a healthy percentage.

When I explained that to the president of this financial services company, the advice gave him much more clarity on the issue and prompted him to shift the energies of the financial advisors, who had taken their eyes off the ball.

The advice came out of my lessons learned in the investment banking world, where I had been guilty of becoming bogged down with potential clients who were never going to come through, which I could have realized if I had read their signals correctly. It wasn't until those of us in charge of our investment bank sat down and talked through what our ideal clients looked like and how we were spending our time that our business focus and profitability improved. What helped was formulating a list of questions and then working our way through them:

1. Who are your ideal clients?
2. What is the size of their company, net worth, or transaction size?
3. Are they high maintenance?
4. Do they pay their bills?
5. Do they understand the value you bring to their company?
6. Can you hit your targeted gross margin or percentage return on investment (ROI) with these clients?
7. Can you grow with them?

---

8. Do you have the products and services to handle their needs and wants?

9. Can you alleviate or reduce their pain?

It's important to step back and continuously reassess your offering. It's easy to lose sight of your core offering and lose sight of who your ideal client is, especially in this age, when companies take any business that walks through the front door.

HAVE, DO, AND BE

To help you approach everything you do with a level of clarity, I'd like to introduce you to concept called the *have, do, and be list,* which was a tool introduced to me by Jack Canfield, a friend and author of the *Chicken Soup for the Soul* series. The have, do, and be list has helped me create and manifest things in my life that I never thought were possible. In a sense, the have, do, and be list is about the art of manifestation in your career, business, and life.

What is the have, do, and be list? The *have* includes things you want to have in your life. They could be attaining possessions, such as a home, a new car, or some other material goods.

The *do* refers to things you want to do in your life or that you would be excited about, such as skydiving or flying as a passenger in an F-16 fighter jet. They can be altruistic, such as volunteering on a medical missions trip to a developing country, or they can be related to achieving your business goals.

The *be* refers to the type of person you want to become, such as grateful, energetic, or respected by others.

I look at my have, do, and be list every day. The items on it number 90 (30 in each category). When I complete a task, or feel like an item is no longer an objective, I highlight it and add more.

Why does this process work so well? Because defining the tasks you need to or must complete, making a list you can refer to, and prioritizing them helps break down larger goals into smaller tasks and maintain focus. Seeing your *have, do,* or *be* item in your handwriting or onscreen becomes an impetus to action.

The inspiration for something on your have, do, and be list can come from anywhere. One example came from my admiration for the U.S. Navy SEALs. Several years ago, I read *Lone Survivor: The Eyewitness Account of Operation Redwing and the Lost Heroes of SEAL Team 10* by Marcus Luttrell. Learning what these elite warriors did captivated me and prompted me to wonder what it would be like to get a real taste for what they go through as they prepare themselves for dangerous missions. I even wondered if there was a Navy SEAL retreat for business executives, but I couldn't find any fantasy weekends. I did find out about a grueling two-week audition, but that's for 19-year-olds thinking of putting themselves through six months of pure hell to see whether they have what it takes to be a Navy SEAL.

Even though there wasn't anyplace where I could get a hands-on experience with special forces, I added "a training session with the Navy SEALs" to my have, do, and be list because of my respect for the men and women in the military who are willing to give up their lives to preserve and protect our freedoms. Because of that commitment, *Anything for the military* is my motto. Whenever I've been asked to speak to soldiers, I clear my schedule.

A couple of years ago, a colonel at Fort Sheridan, a military installation on Lake Michigan, asked me to speak to 400 troops returning from Iraq and Afghanistan about the transition from military life to civilian life (Figure 6.3). I immediately said yes and prepared a talk titled "Tradition in Transition." I told the soldiers in attendance that our code words were *Operation Crossover*. I wanted to inspire the troops returning from overseas and provide them practical advice for transitioning from military life to a civilian work environment.

Joe Musselman, founder of the Honor Foundation in San Diego, a start-up that helps special operations personnel transition

FIGURE 6.3 **"Tradition in Transition" talk with returning troops from Afghanistan and Iraq at Fort Sheridan, Illinois**

from military service to a career in the private sector, heard about my talk and was intrigued.

We had a great chat on the phone, and then he called a month later with some exciting news. The University of California, San Diego (UCSD), had given the Honor Foundation 10,000 square feet of classroom space on the UCSD campus at no charge. Joe got to work establishing a curriculum that would help Navy SEALs and other elite soldiers make the transition to the private sector by providing training and resources to secure a job. He had a hole in his curriculum that he was looking to fill. Joe asked me to teach a course on networking and career development, similar to what I did at Fort Sheridan.

That was an easy yes.

When I stood in front of some of America's finest in San Diego, I started off by saying, "Gentlemen, we are at war. We are at war with wasted talent." I explained that the U.S. unemployment rate hovers at 7 percent but the U.S. ex-military has an unemployed rate nearly double that at 13 percent. Military personnel between the ages of 18 and 30 who were recently discharged face an unemployment rate of 28 percent.

"The fact is, we need you in the private workforce," I said. "We've seen a lot of business scandals in recent years. In 1980, 60 percent of CEOs had military experience, while in 2013 only 8 percent of CEOs have military experience. That's why I want to help take you from protecting America to building America, from the ship deck to the shipping dock, from the battlefield to the sales field, from hero to hire."

I talked about the importance of relationships and how the relationships we forge are the most significant factor in achieving success and happiness in business and in life. I explained that networking—and helping others—leads to establishing relationships, which leads to business development.

During my two days of teaching at the Honor Foundation, I was fortunate to get a private tour inside of the Naval Special Warfare Command in nearby Coronado. Highlights were tackling a military obstacle course where I climbed the 30-foot rope wall and fired an automatic weapon at a shooting range. (I am not sure I'm quite SEAL material yet.) (Figure 6.4)

My respect for the SEALs was high before my visit, but after spending three days with them out in San Diego, my admirations and esteem have grown exponentially for the Navy SEALs. I left Coronado with three important lessons:

1. *Be prepared versus thinking you are prepared and ready.* The Basic Underwater Demolition/SEAL (BUD/S) training puts candidates through the most physical and psychological training possible. I was there during Day 4 of their six-month course. I was told that out of 160 candidates, 61 recruits had quit—after spending years preparing for their chance to become a Navy SEAL.

   Every one of those 160 candidates thought he was prepared, but nearly a hundred were clearly not ready. The work you put into the front end helps you on the back end.

FIGURE 6.4   Training on the obstacle course at the Naval Special Warfare Command in Coronado, California

2. *Have a big enough why.* There's no doubt these warriors believe so strongly in the cause of freedom that they are willing to give their lives to protect our liberties and freedoms. Any Navy SEAL is an instant hero in my book. Is my why in life as big as theirs? Probably not, but I could learn from them about commitment, trust, camaraderie, and duty.

3. *Have a clear laserlike focus.* The SEALs always have a clear objective when it comes to fulfilling a mission. They are able to focus their energies entirely on the goal at hand because they follow a time-tested system that stretches them and takes the SEALs to places they never thought they could go. I can do that, too.

My time spent teaching and interacting with elite military personnel in San Diego was an example of how the have, do, and be list worked for me. Consider putting this tool into your playbook as well. If you write down five items in each of the *have, do,* and *be* categories, that would be a great start (Figure 6.7).

It's okay if some of your *have, do,* and *be* desires are bucket list items. Besides wanting to meet and hang out with the Navy SEALs, one of my *do* items was flying in a F-16 Fighting Falcon fighter jet à la Tom Cruise from *Top Gun.*

But guess what? Just as a fantasy weekend with the Navy SEALs was out of the question, so was finding a ride in the second seat of a frontline U.S. Air Force fighter jet capable of roaring down the runway in an explosion of thrust and rocketing into the heavens at twice the speed of sound at 1,500 miles per hour.

I kept visualizing this experience in my mind, so much so that I could even smell the burning jet fuel and feel the heat of the afterburner on the back of my head when I pretended I was in the backseat of a fighter jet. I made it a daily practice to imagine myself in the act of flying a fighter jet.

The story came full circle when I was asked to speak at Govig and Associates, an executive recruiting firm in Phoenix, about business development and networking. Todd Govig, the president, had become a really good friend, so I waived my customary fee.

A few weeks later, I saw Todd at a CEO networking event in Phoenix. I was talking with Todd about setting goals and described the *have, do,* and *be.* I had my planner with me and flipped to the back, where I kept my own list, including how I wanted to fly in an F-16 someday.

Todd appraised my list, then said, "Wow, that's really cool."

A few days later, after I returned to Milwaukee, Todd called and said he had good news for me. "I can get you into an L-39 Albatros," he said. "It's a Czech-built fighter jet that's similar to the F-16s. The Albatros is the most widely used fighter jet trainer in the world. It looks like one of those Russian MiG fighters."

I was wondering whether that meant I had to fly to Prague or Moscow when Todd interrupted my thoughts.

"My best friend's best friend is Dan Sullivan. He's a successful entrepreneur from Minnesota. He sold his medical device company and bought himself an L-39 fighter jet. If you can get back to Minneapolis next Tuesday morning, you've got a ride in an Albatros."

Dan was one of the coolest guys I have ever met. He belonged to a group known as the Air Hoppers—five entrepreneurs who decided to buy Eastern Bloc fighter jets—complete with Soviet-era red stars emblazoned on the fuselage—and take the sleek fighter around the country to air shows. (You can learn more at www.hopperflight.com.) They also sold rides on the swept-wing jet with a long, pointed nose leading back to a tandem cockpit, in which the pilot and passenger sat under individual canopies.

Dan took me through the preflight briefing.

The takeoff was fine. I kept breakfast down through some loops, rolls, and Immelmann turns.

We were at cruising altitude when I heard Dan in my headset: "Joe, you want to fly this?"

I gently put my hand around the throttle. Dan lifted his hands into the air.

"Push the stick forward an eighth of an inch," he directed.

I did, and the whole plane tipped rapidly forward.

Somehow, I managed to stay conscious as my stomach lurched and bounced around like a Powerball. I still thoroughly enjoyed myself, however. When we landed after a 40-minute ride and I emerged from the cockpit, I needed help finding my land legs (Figure 6.5).

I had a huge smile on my face, though. That epic experience never would have happened if I hadn't had a have, do, and be list in my life and if I hadn't shared it with others.

FIGURE 6.5   Joe Sweeney finding his land legs with "Lieutenant" Dan Sullivan after a Flight on the L39 Albatros

What about you?

What are some things you would like to have, do, and be in your life? The possibilities are up to you. Creating your own have, do, and be list will help you identify goals, develop a strategy to reach them, and achieve a happier and more fulfilling life.

If You Want to Be Happy...

Lou Holtz, who used to coach Notre Dame football and is now a college football commentator on the Entertainment and Sports Programming Network (ESPN), shared his formula for a happy life. In a talk I heard him give, he was riffing on happiness and fulfillment in life and how the only real path to happiness was to serve others consistently.

Then Holtz expanded on that thought with this great list:

- If you want to be happy for an hour, eat a steak.
- If you want to be happy for a day, play a round of golf.
- If you want to be happy for a week, go on a cruise.
- If you want to be happy for a month, buy a car.
- If you want to be happy for a year, win the lottery.
- If you want to be happy for a lifetime, figure out how to add value to the lives of others and serve them.

Joe's Recap

Getting Clear by Creating Your Ideal Day and Ideal Life

- Bob Buford, in his book *Halftime: Moving from Success to Significance,* writes that at some point in your life, it's important to pause and consider how to make the transition to living your ideal life.
- Buford says that visualizing where you want to be, what you want to be doing, and who you would like to be doing it with are key to living an ideal life.
- Besides planning for next week, you could also think about planning for the next year. A good time to reflect on what you want to do in the next year is during the holiday season between Thanksgiving and Christmas.
- Using either your smartphone or a planner, schedule any big business trips, people you need to see, board meetings you need to lock in, strategic alliances you need to make, and any personal plans, such as family vacations.
- Planning your ideal life is important, but few ever think that far ahead. Most people devote more thought to planning their next vacation than to planning their ideal

(continued)

(*continued*)

    lives. You'll benefit greatly if you set aside even a short time to visualize what your ideal life would look like.

- Creating a have, do, and be list will be a powerful tool you can use to accomplish your goals. The *have* refers to the things you want to have in your life. The *do* refers to things you want to do in your life or that you would feel good about. The *be* refers to who you would like to be or what you want to be known for.

- A key element in the development of your have, do, and be list is engaging in *active daydreaming*. This exercise is about manifesting people, events, and things into your life.

- Some of your *have, do,* and *be* desires could be very long-term goals. What's important is having things to shoot for as you try to live your ideal life.

Exercises

1. Using Figure 6.1 from this chapter, describe what an ideal day would look like.

       The point of this exercise is to help you identify the activities that need to be in your day in your ideal day. Once you define the smaller tasks you need to accomplish every day and make working on these tasks a daily habit, you'll see how the power of effective habits helps you progress toward achieving your goals.

       Start by describing your ideal day hour by hour. You may want to refer to your Winning Action Plan in Chapter 1 and your Decision Wheels in Chapter 2 before you start writing.

2. Next, define an ideal week. If you had 20 minutes to plan your week on a Sunday afternoon, what would it look like? Twenty minutes of planning on Sunday afternoon will save you several hours during the week.

You might have a FEW meeting—plan *food*/meals for the week, organize your *exercise* time, and remember to stay hydrated with *water*.

This would also be a good time to revisit your Life Decision Wheels to make sure you're keeping all the plates spinning during the week. Are you doing something to advance each area of your life this week? Are you making decisions that enable you to keep the plates spinning?

Week of: _____

Food: _____

Exercise: _____

Water: _____

3. After you define your ideal week, it's time to tackle your ideal month. Refer to Figure 6.2 from this chapter.

   What are some things you would like to see happen monthly in each area?

   _____

   _____

   _____

4. The period between Thanksgiving and New Year's Day is an excellent time to begin planning for the next year. Write down five big goals or tasks that you want to accomplish in the coming year.

   1.

   2.

   3.

   4.

   5.

5. Using Figure 6.6, write an entire page on what the ideal life would look like to you. Describe where you would be and what you would be doing.

(continued)

(continued)

What would your life look like if it really turned out great?

Write one full page in detail.

FIGURE 6.6   The Ideal Life

6. Here is a list of questions to help you identify your ideal client:

    a. Who are your ideal clients?

    _____

    _____

    b. What is the size of their company, net worth, or transaction size?

    _____

    _____

    c. Are they high maintenance?

    _____

    d. Do they pay their bills?

    _____

    e. Do they understand the value you bring to the transaction?

    _____

    f. Can you hit your targeted gross margin or percentage ROI with these clients?

    _____

    _____

    g. Can you grow with them?

    _____

    _____

    h. Can you add value?

    _____

    i. Can you alleviate their pain?

    _____

7. Complete this Life Planning form (Figure 6.7). What are some things you would love to have, would desire to do, or would love to be?

(continued)

(continued)

Life Planning		
Have	Do	Be
New convertible	Run half marathon	More appreciative and grateful

FIGURE 6.7   Life Planning

SECTION

Get Free

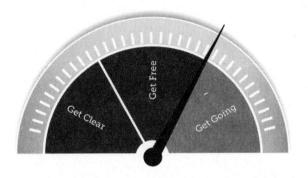

Get clear, get free, and get going.

The second aspect of the formula—get free—is an important step because after you get clear, you really can't get going until you get free. Getting free is all about creating the proper mind-set when interacting with people, planning activities, managing money, and looking at life, as well as eliminating self-limiting thoughts. As Dr. Wayne W. Dyer says, "When you change the way you look at things, the things you look at change." With the proper mind-set, you can create a bridge that can take you from getting clear to getting going.

One of the major reasons why people can't get free is because they have various memes influencing them on a subconscious level. What is a meme? A meme, according to the Urban Dictionary, is an idea, belief, "or pattern of behavior that spreads throughout a culture either vertically by cultural inheritance (from parents to children) or horizontally through the culture (from peers, social media, or popular entertainment).[1]

A common meme is that if you grow up, go to college, get a good job, get married, raise 2.3 kids, and own a home, then you'll be happy. Another meme is the more money you make, the more things you can buy, which also brings satisfaction and happiness.

We all have dozens of memes lodged in our thoughts, but some people can't get free because of the memes they carry around with them. How do I know? By talking with thousands of people over the years. I've heard people say they are trying to get free, but they carry negative thoughts around:

- I'm not very smart because I got Cs in high school and college.
- I've been stuck in one dead-end job after another.
- Managers never want to promote me.
- I make one mistake after another.
- If I make more money and close more deals, then I will be happy.
- Once I find my perfect partner, then my life will find some order.

In this section, we'll explore how to deal with the various memes in your life as well as other areas that hold all of us back from getting free and reaching our potential.

CHAPTER 7

Get Free by Taking 100 Percent Responsibility

Get Free

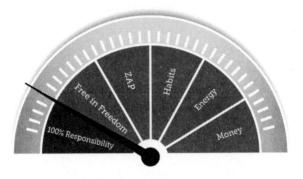

Most people do not really want freedom because freedom involves responsibility, and most people are frightened of responsibility.

—SIGMUND FREUD, from his book *Civilization and Its Discontents*[1]

A man named Charlie is on his deathbed in the hospital and has only a few days to live.

Turning to his wife, he says, "Martha, I have been doing a lot of thinking about my life and you have always been there. When I dropped out of college, you were there. When I lost my first job, you were there. When I lost my second job, you were still there. When I lost all of our money and our house, you were there. When we moved into our efficiency apartment, you were there. And now that I am dying of cancer, I have concluded, after all these years … Martha, you're just *bad* luck!"

You could make the case that Charlie never took responsibility for anything that happened to him. So let me ask you this: How responsible are you for what happens in your life?

Is it 50/50?

How about 52/48?

Or 60/40?

Of course, the answer is that you are 100 percent responsible for everything that happens in your life. Until you accept this basic fact, you will never get entirely *free*.

I know there are things out of our control. But taking personal responsibility for the aspects you *can* control and taking responsibility for what happens in your life—good, bad, or indifferent—will also make you more accountable for the choices you make.

My Favorite Movie Clip of All Time

Whenever I speak on the topic of getting free, I play a clip from one of the greatest movies of all time— *Braveheart*.

If you've seen the film starring Mel Gibson as thirteenth-century Scottish warrior William Wallace, then you know the famous scene. In the climactic Battle of Bannockburn, Wallace—his face painted in blue-and-white stripes—fired up his ragtag troops as he moved about on his stallion, yelling that the English may take their lives but never their freeeeeeedoooom!

Wallace believed in the pursuit of freedom so much that it became his life's mission and ultimate passion. The Scotsman believed that you haven't lived or found real freedom until you believe in a cause so much that you are willing to die for it.

My parents created a home where all nine sons and one daughter were responsible for getting themselves up on time and getting ready for school, preparing their own breakfast and sack lunch, arriving at school on time ... and that was just the first hour of the day! In such an environment, I learned to rely on myself, not in a sense that I was on my own, but in a sense I was being raised in a warm, loving home where I was expected to do my part to make the entire family unit thrive.

By teaching all their children to be responsible, my parents were also teaching me to take responsibility. Little did I know then that they were giving me a wonderful gift that has enriched my life and filled me with a sense of freedom.

As Abraham Lincoln, the sixteenth president of the United States, said one time, "You cannot escape the responsibility of tomorrow by evading it today."

A PhD IN ENTITLEMENT

Father Richard Rohr, a Franciscan priest from Albuquerque, New Mexico and a popular spiritual writer and retreat leader, says in his talks and in his book *The 12 Steps of Emotional Sobriety* that to be born in America today—and, by extension, any developed country—is like receiving a PhD in entitlement. Many people no longer take responsibility for their actions. Instead, they feel like they deserve everything they can get their hands on because society owes them.

The problem with believing you deserve a certain outcome can lead to anger, frustration, and ultimately unhappiness. If you have some resentment at the government, your parents, or your employer because you think you're owed something or didn't have the same opportunities everyone else got, then take inventory of everything you have in your life and focus on what you have rather than what you *should* have. Go from *entitlement to gratitude!*

So the question becomes: What *can* you be grateful for?

Thoughts on Entitlement

Rev. William John Henry Boetcker, a Presbyterian minister who lived from 1873 to 1962, wrote these aphorisms in a pamphlet titled *Lincoln on Limitations* that seem just as apropos today:

You cannot bring about prosperity by discouraging thrift.

You cannot strengthen the weak by weakening the strong.

You cannot help the wage earner by pulling down the wage payer.

You cannot further the brotherhood of man by encouraging class hatred.

You cannot help the poor by destroying the rich.

You cannot keep out of trouble by spending more than you earn.

You cannot build character and courage by taking away man's initiative and independence.

You cannot help men permanently by doing for them what they could and should do for themselves.[2]

Sure, we're appreciative to be alive or in good health, but that's where it ends for many folks. There's a lot of resentment out there for all sorts of reasons, so if there is any resentment seeping out of your pores, then all you have to do is go back in history to realize how grateful we all can be for living in the twenty-first century.

THE 200-YEAR RULE

Whenever I speak to college audiences, I like to tell them, "Anytime you're unappreciative or feeling like you got a bad break, go back 200 years."

I call it my 200-Year Rule.

I used to grumble about going to the doctor for my little aches and pains. I hated giving blood because I never liked needles. That is, until I read several books about the Civil War and learned how they treated battlefield injuries. With no anesthesia except for a swig of whiskey, doctors sawed off limbs left and right. If you got shot in the knee, they hacked your leg off. The greatest surgeons were the ones who sawed the fastest.

I recently got my first cavity in 35 years. I was anxious when I had to lie back in the dentist's chair and get my tooth drilled, but if you went to a dentist 200 years ago, they took one look at that hole in your tooth and yanked the tooth out with a wrench. Without Novocain!

When I read *Undaunted Courage: The Pioneering First Mission to Explore America's Wild Frontier* by Stephen E. Ambrose, I was fascinated to learn about Lewis and Clark's momentous 1803 expedition up the Missouri River to the Rockies, over the mountains, and down the Columbia River to the Pacific Ocean. I admired the way they chopped down trees to make dugout canoes to navigate the rivers.

I was thinking about the supreme difficulty of Lewis and Clark's journey—no roads, no 7-Elevens, and no Motel 6 rooms along the way—when I got into my four-door sedan one snowy morning. Ah, the luxury: heated seats, heated steering, and a cup holder for my hot coffee as I started the morning commute. The local news that morning was all about the terrible 6-inch snowstorm in Milwaukee and how local residents were urged to stay inside. *Storm watch! Don't leave your house!*

I wondered what Lewis and Clark would have thought if they were listening to the same news advisory that day. I know exactly what they would have said: We're a bunch of softies. So I have a new rule: I don't care if there is 3 feet of snow on the ground, I'm driving to work that day.

Louis Szekely, known professionally as Louis C.K., is an acerbic comedian. He captured this lack of perspective about how much we have to be grateful for with his riff on Comedy Central about griping air travelers. If you think about it, a lot of folks have lost perspective on how amazing commercial flight actually is[3]:

Whiny passenger: And then, we got on the plane, and they made us sit there on the runway for a whole 40 minutes. We just sat there, not moving at all.

Louis C.K.: Oh, really? What happened next? Did you fly through the air incredibly, like a bird? Did you partake in the miracle of human flight and then land softly on giant tires? People say there are delays on flights. Really? You flew from New York to California in 5 hours. Try going there in a covered wagon. That used to take months at one time. Plus, there was a good chance that you and your family could die on the way.

Think about it. Now you're sitting in a chair 40,000 feet in the air, going 550 miles per hour! That's the stuff of Greek mythology, so don't complain about the hassles and inconveniences of air travel to me.

Louis C.K. makes a good point, but here's the deal: *Gratefulness can help set you free.* Understanding how good you have it today—with all the modern conveniences, computerized gadgets, and technological advancements—should give you a positive attitude and a sunny disposition, which is a big part of getting free. All you have to do is look back and study history a bit to realize how fortunate you are to live in times like this.

The Paradox of Our Time

We have taller buildings but shorter tempers;
Wider freeways but narrower viewpoints;
We spend more but have less;
We buy more but enjoy it less;
We have bigger houses and smaller families;
More conveniences, yet less time;

> We have more degrees but less sense;
> More knowledge but less judgment;
> More experts, yet more problems;
> More medicine, yet less wellness.
> —Dr. Bob Moorehead, former church pastor[4]

EVERY DAY IS A BONUS

If you've never served in the military, then looking to our men and women in uniform as well as our brave veterans from past wars should fill your breast with gratitude for ensuring our freedoms.

During the Memorial Day weekend of May 2013, I was invited to a local fund-raising event for Stars and Stripes Honor Flight, which raises money to send World War II, Korean War, and terminally ill veterans from Milwaukee to Washington, DC, where they can visit inspirational war memorials before they pass away.

Since 2008, Stars and Stripes Honor Flight has flown more than 1,800 veterans from southeast Wisconsin to our nation's capital at no charge to them. The success of the Wisconsin effort spurred Stars and Stripes Honor Flight to turn this into a national program with 110 hubs in 34 states.

The fund-raiser that Memorial Day weekend coincided with the showing of *Honor Flight*, a documentary about the initiative to honor World War II vets. This wasn't any ordinary film screening at a local theater in Cedarburg, Wisconsin. *Honor Flight*, as you would expect, was quite emotional and moving. One of the four veterans chronicled in the film was Joe Demler, an 87-year-old, soft-spoken retired postmaster.

Joe was captured during the Battle of the Bulge in December 1944 and shipped to Stalag 12-A in Limburg, Germany. This was toward the end of the war, and the prisoners were treated horribly. There was very little food for the German population and even less for Allied prisoners.

Joe and his fellow prisoners were starved. When the Allies liberated his prisoner camp on April 10, 1945, a *Life* magazine photographer snapped a picture of him lying on his bunk. His emaciated body looked frighteningly similar to those of Hitler's concentration camp victims. The 19-year-old soldier weighed 67 pounds.

That photo was featured in *Life* magazine and became one of the most unforgettable images of World War II. Joe would forever be known as the Human Skeleton.

Over the years, I've seen that photo thousands of times.

Why can I say thousands?

Because my parents kept that issue of *Life* magazine on a stand in our living room. They wanted all 10 of their children to understand the price of freedom.

FIGURE 7.1   Joe Demler holding the *Life* magazine with his image on the cover. He weighed 67 pounds when the allies liberated his prisoner camp in 1945

FIGURE 7.2 "Every Day is a Bonus" is the motto of the Stars and Stripes Honor Flight. It is also the mantra that kept him alive in the German POW camp

Here's what most people miss about that dramatic photo in *Life* magazine. If you look closely, you see another prisoner to Joe's right, who looks much healthier.

That prisoner didn't make it. He died shortly after the prisoners were liberated because he had basically given up. Joe, on the other hand, had a different mind-set because he learned two things in a Nazi prison camp: how to pray and how every day he lived was a bonus.

I got to meet this hero at the screening of *Honor Flight* and shake his hand. This brave soldier experienced a freedom that few of us will ever experience. On his ball cap was the phrase he lived by: *Every Day Is a Bonus*.

The key is a grateful heart, so if you really want to be free, then remind yourself to start living in a state of gratitude today—something Joe Demler has been doing since an April day in 1945.

So, let me close with this thought: We live in the greatest time in human history. You can make the most of the life ahead of you—and get free—when you believe in three things:

1. Tomorrow will be better than today.
2. You can have a positive impact on the future.
3. You'll benefit when you assume 100 percent responsibility.

Joe's Recap

Get Free by Taking 100 Percent Responsibility

- How responsible are you for what happens in your life? Until you realize this basic fact of complete responsibility, you will never get entirely *free*.
- Take personal responsibility for the things you *can* control.
- Unless you want to be part of a culture of dependency, then you have to take responsibility for your what's happening in your life—good, bad, or indifferent.
- Anytime you're unappreciative or feeling like you got a bad break, go back 200 years.
- Every day is a bonus, so live that way. If you've never served in the military, then looking to our men and women in uniform as well as our brave veterans from past wars should fill your breast with gratitude for ensuring our freedoms.

Exercises

1. We all have memes or self-talk swirling in our brains. What memes are holding you back? (Examples would be: *I should have more money ... I should have greater success ... Why aren't my kids doing better?*)

   _____

   _____

   _____

2. What are the five things you are most grateful for in your life?

 1.

 2.

 3.

 4.

 5.

3. What are the things that you feel like you've taken responsibility for in your life?

_____

_____

_____

CHAPTER **8**

Your Perspective Determines Your Freedom

Get Free

> How do you see the world? The great danger is to fall into the trap of believing that the whole world is like the city we live in. The temptation is to fall into the subconscious lethargy of thinking that the whole world is like the street we live on.
>
> —MATTHEW KELLY, author of *The Rhythm of Life: Living Every Day with Passion and Purpose*[1]

How you choose to see the world also influences how you begin each day, how you interact with the people you meet, and how you make decisions throughout the day. With the proper perspective, you'll see a lot more opportunities in your life—and experience freedom.

Many people who can't get free struggle with negative attitudes or fear of taking control of or responsibility for their lives.

So how do you see the world?

Author Matthew Kelly asks that question at the start of this chapter. Instead of falling into the trap of believing that the whole world is like the neighborhood you live in, Kelly writes in his book *The Rhythm of Life* that if you reduced the world's population of 7 billion to 100 people, things would shake out proportionally in this manner:

- Fifty-seven would come from Asia.
- Twenty-one would come from Europe.
- Fourteen would come from North America *and* South America.
- Eight would come from Africa.
- Fifty-one would be women; 49 would be men.
- Sixty-eight would not be able to read and write.
- Six would own or control almost 50 percent of the world's wealth, and of those six people, five would be U.S. citizens.
- Only one would have gone to college.
- One would have been recently born, and one would be about to die.
- Of those dying soon, one-third would die from a lack of bread, one-third would die from a lack of justice, and one-third would die from overeating (or obesity-related diseases).

So, how do you see the world? One-quarter of all humans live without electricity, 15 percent lack adequate access to clean drinking water, and 2 billion people, or 30 percent of the global population, live on less than $2.50 a day.

I share these sobering insights because the way we see the world determines our attitudes. Our attitudes determine the way we live our lives. And the way we live our lives determines how much freedom we feel.

A NEW GIFT OF FREEDOM

You could say that my father, Ray Sweeney, lived the life that he expected. First, he was among the "Greatest Generation" who came of age in the 1940s. Under the cultural norms of the day, he was expected to find a nice girl and settle down, raise a family with lots of kids underfoot, stay with his trade or career for the next 45 years, and then retire at age 65 with a pension and a gold watch.

For the most part, my father followed that path. He and my mother managed to feed, clothe, and raise a family of 10 energetic kids. He owned and operated the same plumbing, heating, and wholesale business his whole life. When he got into his fifties and sixties, he always knew what he'd be doing the day he turned 65—kicking up his feet, ruffling the newspaper, and letting someone else do the work.

We don't live like that anymore. For openers, we can't. The days of punching a time clock for the same company your entire working life ended with the demise of the Industrial Age and the emergence of the computerized Information Age. In turn,

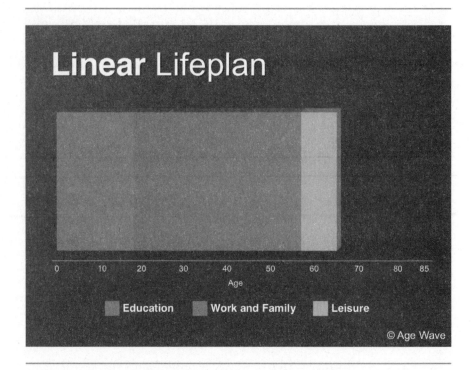

FIGURE 8.1   Ken Dychtwald's Linear Lifeplan

companies had to adapt to rapid changes in manufacturing and distribution, and those that didn't adapt were soon shuttered. That's the main reason why no one maintains the same career for 40 or 50 years.

The other big societal shift is the longevity bonus from our increased life expectancy, which new breakthroughs in medicine have aided. During the Roman Empire, average life expectancy at birth was only 22 years. By 1900, life expectancy had doubled, but not by much as people lived to be 47 years of age. Then during the twentieth century, there was an unprecedented and rapid rise in life expectancy from advances in modern medicine as well as the wide availability of nutritious foods. Today, the average life expectancy is 78.7 years for both sexes, according the Centers for Disease Control and Prevention.

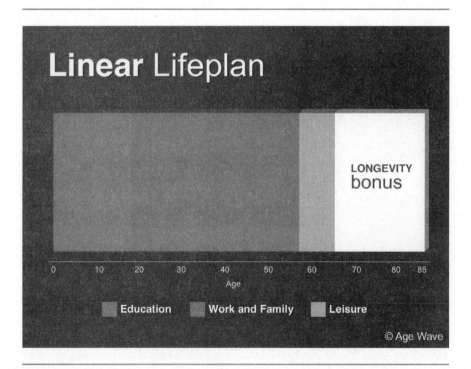

FIGURE 8.2   Ken Dychtwald's Linear Lifeplan with Longevity Bonus

Because we have 30 more years to live than we did a century ago, what are we going to do with them? No matter your age, you have an excellent chance of having more time to do many things in life and explore areas that interest you. Just because you're doing something today doesn't necessarily mean you'll be doing that in the future.

In light of the freedoms that come with living longer, Ken Dychtwald, the founder and chief executive officer of Age Wave and the author of 16 books, says there's a new trend of people going back to school in their fifties and starting new careers. Previous generations never did that because they lived *linear* lives, meaning they grew up and went to school for the first two decades of their lives, worked and raised a family for the next 40 years, and then went out to pasture in their sixties. They spent the last few years of their lives reaping the rewards of working hard.

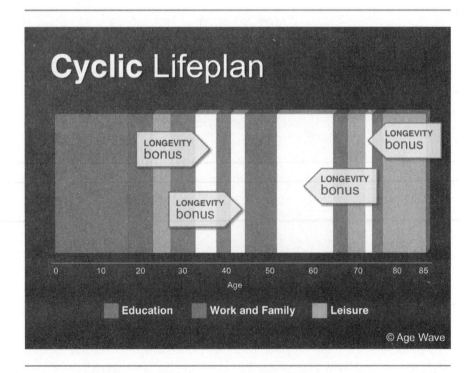

FIGURE 8.3   Ken Dychtwald's Cyclic Lifeplan

That's all changing now.

"What's replacing the linear life plan is a cyclic life plan, in which people are continually reinventing themselves and trying new things," Dychtwald said in an interview with *JWT Intelligence*, the website of JWT, an international marketing firm. This trend, in a way, erases a lot of the expectations of what you're supposed to do when you hit a certain age. Dychtwald's declaration that people can pursue passions and possibly reinvent themselves can also be incredibly freeing. Longevity of life allows you to follow your passions and launch new endeavors. No matter what your age is, your perspective on life will determine your freedom.

> ### Words to Live By
>
> It's never too late to have a happy childhood. But the second one is up to you and no one else.
>
> —Regina Brett, columnist[2]

Joe's Recap

Your Perspective Determines Your Freedom

- How you perceive the world influences how you live your life, how you interact with the people you meet, and what decisions you make throughout the day.
- Life is like rafting down a twisting, turning white-water river, but what's different today is the length of the trip because of increased life expectancy.
- Because of added life expectancy, we have 30 more years to live than we did a century ago. What are we doing to do with them?

Exercises

1. Where are you in the cycle of life?

_____

_____

_____

(continued)

(continued)

2. Do you view your life on the linear life plan, or are you in the process of reinventing yourself?

_____

_____

_____

3. Are you doing work you love? What would your ideal career be, and what would it take to transition to that?

_____

_____

_____

4. Do you foresee making a change in your career path in the future? Do you have the freedom to do that?

_____

_____

_____

CHAPTER 9

Freedom and the ZAP Concept: Zones, Alignment, and Paradoxes

Get Free

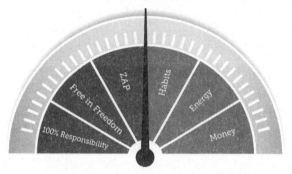

Whatever your work is that produces the greatest abundance and satisfaction, I want you to find it, and I want you to put the highest priority on doing some of it every day.

—GAY HENDRICKS, *The Big Leap: Conquer Your Hidden Fear and Take Life to the Next Level*[1]

Getting free consists of fitting several pieces together so that you can build up the strength to release yourself from negative scripts or faulty beliefs. To assist you in identifying and eliminating these, there are three concepts that will help you find the freedom you desire. Together, they comprise the ZAP concept, which refers to your *z*one of Genius, *a*lignment with others and your goals, and management of the *p*aradoxes in your life and in business.

The ZAP concept is designed to help you get free by first understanding what your zone of Genius is—a term author Gay Hendricks coined in *The Big Leap*. Look for opportunities to work in your zone of Genius as much as you can, and if that means turning off iPhones or not looking at e-mail every 10 minutes so that you can concentrate on writing that report, then that's what you have to do. Changing your habits will help you get clear so that you can next get aligned with your goals. Finally, managing the contradictions so that you're not stuck in a black-and-white world will help you become strong enough to deal with all the paradoxes that come your way.

When you implement all three—the zone of Genius, alignment with others and your goals, and management of the paradoxes in life and business—you become freer in your life, both personally and professionally.

GETTING INTO THE ZONE

Think of the zone of Genius as if it were a sports analogy. As a lifelong sports enthusiast, I appreciate world-class athletes who execute at such a high level that they are said to be *in the zone*. It's like they're unconscious and unaware that they've hit a level of peak performance in which limits seem to fall away. The characteristics of being in the zone include deep concentration, highly efficient performance, emotional buoyancy, a heightened sense of mastery, and a total lack of self-consciousness.

When you think of great athletic performances—Michael Phelps winning 18 gold medals or quarterback Peyton Manning setting the single season record for passing yardage—it's easy to be awed by the immensity of their athletic gifts. These athletes were in a zone where everything flowed, just as they had been trained to do.

We can achieve the same level of excellence. Granted, we can't be in the zone all the time, but we can increase the amount of time we spend in what Hendricks calls your zone of Genius.

When it comes to getting into your zone, the first place to start is with time. Time is the great common denominator: We have the same 24 hours in each day to work with. Time is like a currency, and we can choose to spend it however we want. The difference is that we don't get to roll over any extra time from one day to the next.

When you invest time in a project, you expect a return—just like if you invested money. Here are three gold-plated investments that you may want to consider:

1. Invest in your well-being with proper nutrition, sleep, and exercise. You will gain time and be more productive.
2. Invest in your future by challenging yourself to grow and learn each day.
3. Invest in relationships and in your networks; this is your support system.

Hendricks reinforces this list of investments by saying that we live and work in one of four zones:

- *The Zone of Incompetence*: These are the tasks we are not so good at and don't like doing. We all have to perform duties that we really don't enjoy.

  Many of us have been there and perform well and move up rapidly. There are those who, for whatever reason, get stuck in this zone. People who are stuck and operate mainly in the Zone of Incompetence change jobs a lot because they're operating in a zone where they can't use their talents and gifts.
- *The Zone of Competence*: This is where you are competent and can get the job done. Many people, however, seem content to stay in the Zone of Competence, never stretching themselves to perform beyond the minimum.
- *The Zone of Excellence*: This is when you're doing something you're really good at and you enjoy what you are doing. When you reach this zone, you feel like you're on the right track. Just as child psychologists say it's important for young

children to excel in something—playing the piano, hitting a tennis ball, or writing great stories—it's important for adults to demonstrate proficiency and job skills as well. Excellence is a wonderful quality to have.

Even though it's tempting to ease up and enjoy the ride when you're in the Zone of Excellence, there's one more level where you can truly thrive and show what you're capable of, and that's the Zone of Genius.

- *The Zone of Genius*: When you feel you're doing something you were born to do, then you're in your Zone of Genius. There are periods when we hit our creative sweet spot and the work flows naturally.

Even though you can't be in the Zone of Genius every waking moment, you should be looking for ways to maximize the time there by doing what you are really good at and love to do. What are the skills that allow you to produce huge results in a relatively little amount of time?

Working in your Zone of Genius is about following your purpose and passions and doing what you truly love. You lose track of time when you're in this zone, and you're engaged with your work and happy about the results that flow out of your effort.

In my workshops, I always ask people, "How much time do you spend in your Zone of Genius?"

The answers are all consistent—between 5 percent and 15 percent of their time. If any of us can increase that amount—even double it—we'd see huge results. Think how much you'd accomplish with just 10 percent more of your time in the Zone of Genius.

To increase the amount of time you spend in your Zone of Genius, Hendricks says, you start by answering four questions:

- What do I most love to do?
- What work do I do that doesn't seem like work?
- In my work, what produces the highest ratio of abundance and satisfaction to the amount of time spent?
- What is my unique ability?

If you know what you love to do and what your skill set is, then getting into the Zone of Genius is easy. Begin by clearing your schedule and get to work doing what you love to do or excel at. You want to spend as much time as possible in this zone, keeping distractions to a minimum. Instead of viewing time in a Newtonian manner where the hours and minutes pass uniformly, view time in an Einstein-like manner where space and time are relative, which means *you* decide how to use your time.

Great leaders manage their time by parking themselves in the Zones of Excellence and Genius as long as they can each day.

So I have some questions for you:

- What do you excel at that will help get you into your Zone of Genius?
- Are you able to work in your Zone of Genius at your place of employment, or is it too difficult to get there?
- What are some things that you could do to clear the decks, so to speak, so that you could spend more time in your Zones of Excellence or Genius?

Sometimes, a task as simple as cleaning up the clutter around your workspace is enough to declutter your mind as well. Or you may realize that you do your best work from 7 to 10 AM, or maybe you've discovered that you get a great second wind from 3 to 6 PM.

When I try to help people find their Zone of Genius, I start by asking them to look at their day and write down every task they do. I'll hear responses such as:

- "I'm on the phone constantly from 9 AM to noon; then I have lunch appointments most days."
- "I answer e-mail all morning, have a 2-hour meeting, and then I answer more e-mail."
- "I finally got some time to strategize about next year's budget planning just before I left the office."

The list could go on for pages, but when I study these daily logs, it's common to see 50-hour workweeks where these executives are in their Zone of Genius for 2 hours a week and their Zone of Excellence for perhaps 4 hours. It becomes clear how little time these businesspeople are spending in their Zone of Genius. If you want to do great things, you have to spend time doing things that you are great at and love doing.

It's easy to let days and weeks fill up with chores, tasks, and obligations, but managing time wisely, and delegating when necessary, will free up more time to be in the Zone of Genius. The zone in which you don't want to spend most of your time is the Zone of Competence, where you're managing tasks rather than thinking creatively and innovatively.

Actively maintaining focus on what you're really good at and tracking how much time you're spending in each zone will allow you to establish more time in the Zones of Excellence and Genius. Once you optimize the amount of time you spend in each zone, you can turn your focus to getting aligned and dealing with the paradoxes in your life.

ALIGNMENT AND FREEDOM

The second step in the ZAP formula is getting into alignment. Many times, we struggle to get free because we're out of alignment.

Companies, large and small, get out of alignment all the time. That's why they'll schedule meetings to talk about finding the right strategy to turn things around or stay profitable.

Sure, strategy is critical in businesses. Business executives spend thousands of labor hours to develop an effective strategy, yet they can't seem to get on track or get free. One of the ways that companies can get free is to spend more time improving alignment, rather than developing strategy.

Alignment in business is when everyone is moving in the same direction. It doesn't have to be at the same speed, but everyone needs to be headed on the same path. Your message, your service, your product, and your interaction with customers must all deliver on one promise or value proposition.

I recently had dinner with John McDermott, the Senior Vice President of Global Sales and Marketing for Rockwell International, a $5 billion company. John has thousands of salespeople all over the world. I asked him how he kept the sales force motivated.

"I've been with this company for 32 years, and one of the things I've learned is to focus on alignment. You can have a mediocre strategy with real alignment and be successful because when the alignment is right, momentum can become so strong that it will trump a mediocre strategy any day. Alignment is all about focus, mission, and communication."

I had a question. "Surely with a company with thousands of employees, there has to be more than a few persons who aren't with the program," I commented. "What do you do about them?"

"When you have several thousand employees, you're going to have some bad apples," John agreed. "It's always a matter of how many bad apples before you hit critical mass. If you have a sales staff of 16 people in one department and four or five who don't measure up, that really hurts. That's why alignment demands vigilance from managers."

Here's another example of what I mean by alignment.

Jeffrey Immelt, the Chair and Chief Executive Officer of General Electric (GE), has managed to bring 300,000 employees into alignment. Where Immelt shines is in his ability to connect with people. He consistently communicates GE's core philosophy, goals, and objectives. That's when Immelt is in his Zone of Genius.

If you feel you're out of alignment in your business or personal life, take some time to reread Chapters 1 and 2. Review the questions at the end of each chapter to get back on track and get more clarity regarding the direction you want to go.

MANAGING THE PARADOX

Being a great leader, building or establishing a business, and getting free all require managing the paradoxes in your life.

Executives, managers, and employees cite paradoxes—those propositions in life that sound good but are self-contradictory—as the source of much stress and wasted resources in the workplace. For instance:

- They are tasked with being innovative but at the same time reigning in costs.

  The paradox: To be innovative, it's going to be tough to cut costs.

- They are tasked with thinking strategically with an eye on the future but at the same time, being operationally sound day by day.

  The paradox: How can I be thinking about what we need to be doing in three years when managing the day-to-day takes up the majority of time and resources?

- They are tasked with hitting a certain sales target or production level by a certain date, but they aren't given the resources to do so.

  The paradox: How can I hit my goal if I don't have the resources to make that happen?

Paradoxes: You Can't Live with Them, and You Can't Live without Them

- Cut costs → Be innovative
- Be more efficient → Be more responsive
- Standardize → Customize
- Be secure → Be open
- Deliver predictable service → Be agile
- Execute flawlessly → Think strategically
- Enterprise goals → Business unit goals
- Hurts our division → Helps our company

The question we have to ask ourselves when faced with paradoxes is: How do you determine the real objective, and how you can best deliver on what you are being tasked with? No matter how unrealistic, we need to become strong enough to hold together the contradictions.

Most people take an either/or approach when faced with a paradox. For example: *Do you want me to be innovative, or do you want me to cut costs?* Tasked with doing both, it will be a challenge to do each one effectively.

If you feel like you're faced with an impossible proposition, you should seek support from people you can rely on or who can offer sage advice about managing conflicting demands. The challenge here is to not get caught up by the either/or common in paradoxical situations, but to find ways to deliver a both/and solution by securing support that can help you manage the often conflicting objectives. An in-depth explanation on how to secure support will be covered in Chapter 14.

Joe's Recap

Freedom and the ZAP Concept: Zones, Alignment, and Paradoxes

- This three-step process is designed to help you find the freedom you desire and pinpoint a Zone of Genius where you are aligned with others. This three-step process of getting free is called the ZAP concept, which does three things:
  1. It helps you get into your *Zone of Genius*.
  2. It helps you get *aligned* with others and your goals.
  3. It helps you deal with the *paradoxes* in life and in business.
- When you implement all three—the Zone of Genius, alignment with others and your goals, and management of the paradoxes in life and business—you become freer personally and professionally.

(continued)

(*continued*)

- Gay Hendricks, author of *The Big Leap,* says that we live and work in one of four time zones:
  1. *The Zone of Incompetence*: This is what we are not so good at and don't like doing.
  2. *The Zone of Competence*: This is where you are competent and can get the job done.
  3. *The Zone of Excellence*: This is what you demonstrate proficiency in and enjoy doing.
  4. *The Zone of Genius*: These are skills you have that allow you to produce huge results in a relatively little amount of time.
- Working in your Zone of Genius means following your purpose and passions, doing what you truly love. Time spent in this zone is the most enjoyable, and you're engaged with your work and happy about the results that flow out of your effort.
- Most people spend between 5 and 15 percent of their time in the Zone of Genius. But if you can increase that amount, you'll see huge results.
- The second step in the ZAP formula is getting into alignment. Many times, we struggle to get free because we're out of alignment.
- The final step in the ZAP formula is managing paradoxes. You'll need to secure support that can help you manage the contradictions.

Exercises

1. Do you know when you are in the Zone of Genius? What are you accomplishing when you're in that zone?

   _____

   _____

   _____

Time Zone Tracker		
Task:	What zone am I in? Incompetence Competence Excellence Genius	Amount of time spent in this zone each day:

FIGURE 9.1

(continued)

(*continued*)

2. How many hours a week do you spend in your Zone of Genius? The Zone of Excellence? The Zone of Competence and the Zone of Incompetence? Use the Time Zone Tracker to record how you are spending your time. Study your chart and take steps to spend more time in your Zone of Genius (Figure 9.1).

_____
_____
_____

3. How did you answer the question in the chapter about what you love to do? Are you getting to do what you love to do in your current position?

_____
_____
_____

4. Would you say the company you work for has a workforce where everyone is aligned and is of the same mind? Do you think the employees are aligned?

_____
_____
_____

5. What's the biggest paradox you've experienced in a work setting? How are you dealing with that paradox?

_____
_____
_____

CHAPTER 10

Habits and Getting Free

Get Free

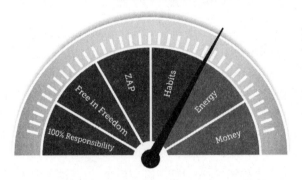

Your beliefs become your thoughts. Your thoughts become your words. Your words become your actions. Your actions become your habits. Your habits become your values. Your values become your destiny.

—MAHATMA GANDHI, Indian leader

Your habits are great predictors of what your life will become because what you do and how you act speak volumes—much more than words.

We all have habits—mannerisms and idiosyncrasies that define what we do and who we are. The habits we choose to nurture are very important because, as Gandhi so eloquently said, they are a reflection of our beliefs, our thoughts, our words, and our actions.

If you want to be in a different place from where you are today in a year, look at and figure out how to change your habits in areas such as your health, your attitude, and your mind. It helps to start by asking the right questions:

- Where am I now?
- Where do I want to go?
- Where do I want to be one year from now? Five years from now?
- What things do I need to change from where I am right now to get where I want to go?

Our habits affect the direction we take and help create clarity in our lives. Whereas bad habits can limit us, good habits set us free because they establish routine, develop a sense of order, and produce efficiency. If you really want to change your life, you start by changing your habits.

If you want to study people with good habits, check out the book *The Blue Zones* by Dan Buettner, who researched the habits and lifestyles of those who have lived the longest from four different cultures around the world.[1] Most of the people he studied lived well into their nineties, and many of them past 100 years. There are a few consistent themes and habits that Buettner noticed regarding the oldest and most fulfilled people on Earth:

1. They put family first.
2. They went outside and exercised daily.
3. They felt a strong sense of purpose and contributed to the common good.
4. They gathered and laughed regularly with friends.
5. They practiced some form of religious or spiritual life.
6. They ate in moderation with plenty of fruits and vegetables in their diet.
7. They stayed active their entire lives.
8. They drank plenty of water.
9. They were always discovering and learning something new.

If you desire to live a long and fulfilling life, you'll want to zero in on four key areas:

- Habits that affect health
- Habits that advance knowledge
- Habits that influence behavior and attitude
- Habits that improve your day

Developing good habits in these four areas will free up time, energy, and resources that were otherwise being expended on bad habits. You won't need to draw on willpower to get things done because over time your discipline will become so ingrained that you *condition* yourself to adopt better, more productive routines. Developing good habits is fundamental to achieving your goals.

Even simple habits play an important role in a person's life. Adopting a new habit, routine, or ritual requires extreme dedication to making it a part of your day. Whereas bad habits are formed very easily, good habits can take much longer to be established. Focusing on changing or establishing one habit at a time, and committing without exception to making it a part of your day, increase the likelihood that the new habit will become part of your daily routine. Although we all know having good habits benefits our health, relationships, and careers, our habits also go a long way toward freeing us up to use our time more effectively, think more critically and creatively, and be more present in the moment.

How can you determine whether your habits are affecting your health, focus, or creativity? How improved would your life be by changing just one habit? Make a list of the habits you have that make you less than your best self. Using a calendar, schedule a period when you will focus, without exception, on replacing one bad habit with a better one. Make note of the changes you see.

The amount of time devoted to actively replacing each habit can vary. Replacing one habit with another is the easiest change to implement. Perhaps you might trade that last hour online for an extra hour's sleep, skip an after work drink in favor of a juice, or identify and eliminate one distraction at work and use that time to develop that new project you've been putting off.

What are the bad habits you want to change or should change? Once you identify some, ask yourself: What is a good habit that can take the place of one of these poor habits? Whether you're aware of it or not, adopting a new routine and staying with it for 30 days means there's a good chance that the new habit will stick with you for a long, long time. Not only are good habits extremely useful as well as healthy, but also, when they're fully integrated into our lives, they free up our minds to concentrate on other activities.

Stephen R. Covey, author of the highly influential business book, *The 7 Habits of Highly Effective People*, writes, "Sow a thought, reap an action; sow an action, reap a habit; sow a habit, reap a character; sow a character, reap a destiny."[2]

MOVING FROM UNHEALTHY TO HEALTHY HABITS

Perhaps the biggest point here—and why so much of this chapter is devoted to physical health—is because the way we feel, the shape we're in, and the moods we have affect every aspect of our lives. Having good health habits gives us more energy, protects us from fatigue, increases our focus, and improves our judgment.

Unfortunately, too many people have bad health habits, such as overeating and consuming junk foods, resulting in obesity. The result of carrying too much weight is affecting too many lives of people on this planet. According to the World Health Organization, in 2008 more than 1.4 billion adults were overweight (of which about 500 million were obese), meaning they weighed at least 50 pounds more than their ideal body weight.[3]

Most of us have struggled to lose weight, but developing new habits that support the lifestyle changes required are some of the most difficult to make. To keep you motivated, remind yourself that your health is a gift and something to be guarded and cherished above all else. If there's an area of your life where you *have* to develop extraordinary habits, it is your health.

Getting rid of negative thoughts, doubt, and rationalizations is essential to developing good habits, making changes in your life, and empowering yourself. Don't listen to the excuses that can stop you from making a major course correction in life, justifications such as:

"I'm too busy."

"I'm too fat."

"I don't have the energy."

"I've got kids."

"I've got parents to take care of."

"I'm going on vacation."

"It costs too much to join a fitness club."

"I can't get motivated."

"I don't have the money."

"Nothing's ever worked before."

Your life will change when you establish good, healthy habits:

- Taking better care of yourself will improve your health and the lives of those who count on you.
- The more you put into it, the more you will receive.
- Putting forth your best effort will yield the best results.
- Establishing good habits will set you free to get going in the right direction, and poor habits will keep you trapped.

When I was an executive with a big stake in a company, my stress and pressure levels were having a negative impact on my health and my family, or so they seemed at the time.

After a long week, I'd have a couple drinks to unwind. Does having a couple of drinks on the weekend have negative consequences on one's life? Many would agree that the answer is no.

But skipping those drinks could have some significant benefits on your health.

I wanted to come up with a better way to deal with stress, so I gave myself a goal: run a marathon. That meant training for several months as I built up my stamina. I traded a bad habit for a good habit. Although I had always associated unwinding with having a drink, I found going for a run or some other exercise after a long week actually helped me unwind, process my day, and get healthy—all while increasing my energy rather than depleting it. Since then, I've run a few marathons, including the Boston Marathon.

Four Areas That Can Increase Your Energy

It takes work to maintain a healthy and fit lifestyle. You must act intentionally in everything you do, paying close attention to these four areas:

1. *Food and nutrition*. Carefully assess and choose what you eat; read nutritional labels, and cook your own foods so as to avoid processed foods.
2. *Activities*. Pursue hobbies and pastimes that keep you active.
3. *Mindfulness*. Pay attention to what you do daily as well as how you're participating in the many communities you are a part of.
4. *Personal development*. What is your true purpose? What is it you want to accomplish most in life? Are you working toward your goals? What do you see as your role in the various personal and professional relationships you have? Are you fulfilling those roles? Do you have an attitude of learning? Are you working toward being better every day?

TAKING INVENTORY

The first step in making a turnaround is setting aside a time of reflection. Are you aware of your habits and how they affect you? Have you thought about what habits you can improve or replace?

Once you have awareness, then you can develop a plan. If you want to change your habits, you must first start recording and measuring everything that influences that habit. If you're concerned about your weight, then record *everything* you eat. If you want to better manage your finances, then record every transaction. If you want to better manage your time, record everything you do in a day, especially the number of hours you spend watching TV or browsing the Web. (Two apps to help with this are loseit.com and mint.com.)

Being more conscious of just what you are eating, buying, or spending time on, and how these choices affect your life, can be illuminating. As nineteenth-century author William James said, "Action may not always bring happiness, but there is no happiness without action."

STAYING ON THE STRAIGHT AND NARROW

I have a quote written down in my planner that I look at every now and then to remind myself to be more conscious of the choices I make. "And yet not choice, but habit rules the unreflecting herd," wrote the nineteenth-century English Romantic poet William Wordsworth.

Getting quiet is a big part of getting clear, getting free, and getting going. Take some time to reflect and ask yourself: What are the habits you have that aren't allowing you to get free? Is it alcohol? Is it drinking too many soft drinks throughout the day? Is it your aversion to exercise or staying up too late so that you can't get to the gym before work? Is it watching too much TV rather than picking up a good book?

When it comes to introducing good habits into your lifestyle, it all starts with making a plan to get there. Reflect on your bad habits and introduce good habits to replace them.

From Soda to Plain Old Water

Five years ago, I traveled to Augusta, Georgia, on a golfing pilgrimage—to witness the Masters Tournament in person. While walking the grounds one day, I ran into Gary D'Amato, a reporter I knew.

I asked him if he wanted to grab some lunch.

"No, I gotta lose some weight," he said, patting his ample stomach. "There's so much food in the press room, and I eat all that crap."

Gary was in his late forties, 6 feet, 1 inch tall. He looked around 230 pounds.

"Do you have something I can write on?" I asked. Gary handed me his notebook, and on a piece of Masters stationery, I wrote the following:

"By August 5, I will feel fit, lean, and alive at 195."

What I did was give Gary some clarity—a goal to shoot for. Now he needed to get free. Since it was April, that meant Gary would have six months to change his diet, change his life, and change his world.

I needed more information, so I asked, "What do you drink during the day? Do you drink any water?"

"Not too much water, but I do like diet cola because of the low calories."

"How many of diet colas do you drink a day?"

"I don't know. Probably four or five."

I smiled.

"Well, maybe it's more than four or five a day," he admitted.

"Tell you what, Gary. When you get home, give me a call, and I'll help you put together a program that will get you back to 195 pounds."

The ball was in his court. To his credit, Gary did reach out to me, which means we were able to get going. The first thing he did was come clean on how many Diet Cokes he was drinking a day. The number was closer to *eight*.

I explained to Gary that we needed to start with baby steps and wean him off diet colas. We went down to six diet drinks a day at the beginning, then four, and then two. Instead of drinking that bubbly diet soft drink, I asked him to drink water, the ultimate calorie-free and sugar-free drink.

Then we rode bikes together in the early morning. He began taking yoga classes. He documented everything he ate and drank. He quickly learned he was consuming many more calories than he realized.

Gary made himself accountable to the hundreds of thousands of readers who read his column by writing about his quest to get back down to 195 pounds, which he accomplished in several months. By recognizing small changes he could make, tracking the details that could help or hurt his progress, and committing to making those changes a part of every day, Gary demonstrated that it's possible to introduce good habits into your life—and reap tremendous results. No matter what your goal is, it really depends on what habits you develop and which ones you jettison.

EDUCATION VERSUS ENTERTAINMENT HABITS

Are you *great* at something—such as playing the piano, windsurfing, crocheting, or even cooking gourmet meals on weekends?

If so, you've likely put 10,000 hours of practice and repetition into your musical instrument, your sport, your hobby, or your kitchen.

The figure of 10,000 hours comes from Malcolm Gladwell, author of the groundbreaking book *Outliers: The Story of Success,* who delved into the backgrounds of successful people from the likes of Bill Gates to John, Paul, George, and Ringo. What he discovered is that greatness in everything from developing computer software to playing the guitar to surfing big waves to dominating a basketball court takes lots and lots of practice—an average of 10,000 hours.

The law of 10,000 hours makes a lot of sense. NBA star Kobe Bryant and golf's Phil Mickelson didn't rise to the top of their professions without putting in an incredible amount of time on the basketball court or driving range. So ask yourself: Where are you putting your hours when you're not working? Are you spending an inordinate amount of time entertaining yourself? The average adult spent more than 5 hours a day either online or using his or her smartphone *and* 4.5 hours a day watching TV in 2013, according to estimates eMarketer released.[4]

So, a few questions:

- Do you attend seminars or classes that relate to your field of work or interest?
- Do you listen to audiobooks?
- Are you keeping up to date on advances in your field with professional journals?
- Do you surround yourself with people who have more experience and greater knowledge than you?
- How much TV do you watch, and what types of shows do you consume?
- How much are you online after work?

Do you have a habit of seeking out entertainment before education? Sure, there are times we should relax, shut down things, sit back, and be amused, but think about how much time you spend on entertainment versus education. If you tend more toward the entertainment side, you can change your life by altering those habits.

It All Adds Up

Have you ever tracked the amount of calories you consume in a day? Many apps and websites make tracking the calories you consume and burn in a day very easy.

The average 12-ounce beer has between 100 and 150 calories, although some local craft ales and lagers easily top 200 calories. But let's say each beer contains 125 calories.

That's 250 calories a night, 1,750 calories a week, or 91,000 extra calories a year. Because a pound of body fat equates to approximately 3,500 calories, that's an extra 26 pounds the body has to deal with.

These extra 91,000 calories a year make it tough to keep the pounds off. Your habits are great predictors of what your life will become because your actions speak more than words.

HABITS OF ATTITUDE

We can all get into the bad habit of having a negative attitude about our careers, our colleagues, our friends, our family, and our life situation. At times it may even feel like a black cloud is following you wherever you go. Rest assured that everybody goes through stormy periods.

Having a good attitude makes us more desirable to be around, whereas habits such as gossiping about others are tough habits to break. If you set your mind to it, though, you can create new habits to guard what you say—new habits that will improve your relationships, establish an impeccable reputation for being honest, and help you maintain a positive mind-set.

I was raised by a mother who told me time after time that if I don't have anything good to say, then don't say it. Before sharing negative comments or passing along some salacious detail, do the GUT Check Test. Step back and ask yourself these three questions:

- Is it good?
- Is it *u*seful?
- Is it *t*ruthful?

If you can't say yes to all three, then don't say it. Let it go.

HABITS TO BEGIN AND END THE DAY

It's important to go to sleep peacefully and start the day peacefully.

The 10 minutes before you to go to sleep are some of the most important in your day. What you do just before you go to bed greatly affects how well and how long you rest because we're all the product of the things we read, the movies we watch, and the TV shows we view before the lights go out.

I think the last few minutes of each day are incredibly important to positive well-being. If you go to bed with scenes of murder and mayhem in your mind after watching an intense movie, your subconscious mind keeps working—and keeps you from getting the rest you need. If you turn off the lights with worry and doubt swirling in your brain, you process those negative thoughts and feelings throughout the night. Instead of getting involved in an action flick or watching car crashes and fires on your local news, I recommend a time of reflection or reading something light, uplifting, and inspirational. *Good thoughts make for good sleep.*

What works for me, just before I go to bed, is sitting down with my journal and answering six questions that are all positive in nature:

1. What was the best thing that happened today?
2. What am I most grateful for today?

3. What did I do to live my ideal day today?
4. What is one new thing I learned today?
5. What did I do to meet my goals today?
6. What am I most looking forward to tomorrow?

Jotting down answers to these thoughtful questions sets me in the right frame of mind for waking up in the morning. Before I adopted this habit, I used to charge out of bed, get the coffee going, collect the morning newspaper, and read e-mails on my home computer.

That's all changed.

Now I leave the newspaper in the driveway and head to my home office—not to check my e-mail, but to spend 5 or 10 minutes of quiet time to get myself clear.

Try grabbing some quiet time first before you do anything else. You'll find that your outlook improves and you will attract positive people and experiences when you take 5 to 10 minutes to reflect on what lies ahead.

I was inspired to make reflection a part of my early morning ritual after reading two biographies about Abraham Lincoln's life—*Team of Rivals* by Doris Kearns Goodwin and *Killing Lincoln* by Bill O'Reilly, which both described what President Lincoln did on the morning he was assassinated—reading the Bible, a habit that he practiced every day for 20 minutes.

Your time of reflection doesn't have to be 20 minutes. Start with 2 minutes. Instead of becoming a chore, you'll find a time of reflection to be one of the most freeing things you can do. Give it a try.

I always end my morning time of reflection by reading an axiom from John Wooden, the University of California, Los Angeles, basketball coach from the 1960s and 1970s. He said, "You can't live a perfect day until you do something for another person who will never be able to repay you."

We all can't live perfect days, but we can go out of our way to do something nice for someone who crosses our path.

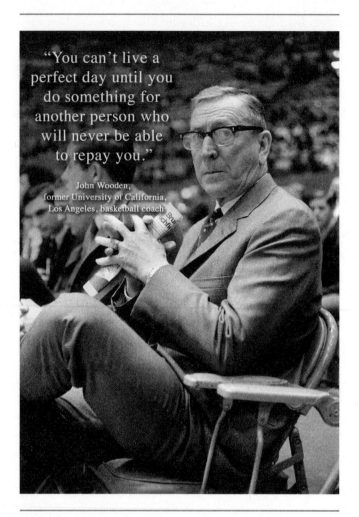

"You can't live a perfect day until you do something for another person who will never be able to repay you."

John Wooden, former University of California, Los Angeles, basketball coach

FIGURE 10.1   John Wooden, former University of California, Los Angeles, basketball coach

OTHER IDEAS WORTH MAKING A HABIT

Good habits can be a game changer in your life.

Just as you can't sharpen knives one time and expect them to remain sharp forever, you can't practice a good behavior one time and expect to see lasting results. You need to sharpen your game continuously by incorporating good habits into your daily life.

Here are some other habits that can greatly improve your life:

1. *Drink plenty of water.* Although there's no hard-and-fast rule on exactly how much water you should drink daily, drinking water is an incredibly healthy practice. According to the Mayo Clinic website, drinking water protects body organs and tissues, lubricates joints, regulates body temperature, carries nutrients and oxygen to cells, and lessens the burden on the kidneys and liver by flushing out waste products.

2. *Get a minimum of 7 hours of sleep.* A good night's rest gives you more energy and helps you think more clearly throughout the day, but the consequences of sleep deprivation are profound: lost productivity, strained interpersonal relationships, and accidents on the road and in the workplace. Sleep is a beneficial yet underappreciated health benefit. The Mayo Clinic affirms that adults who sleep about 7 hours a night have lower mortality rates than those who sleep much more or much less.

3. *Limit alcohol.* Excessive drinking of alcohol has never been a recommended health practice, but drinking modest amounts of wine can improve cardiovascular health by increasing the high-density lipoprotein (HDL) or so-called good cholesterol by 20 percent, if drunk moderately by those who consume a healthy diet and exercise regularly, according to Kathleen M. Zelman at WebMD.

4. *Stay away from diet sodas.* Diet beverages, including chemical sweeteners, have been touted as the answer to America's obesity epidemic for decades, but a 2013 study published in the medical journal *Trends in Endocrinology and Metabolism* concluded that artificial sweeteners are harmful to your health.

5. *Exercise or work out daily.* The benefits of exercise are many. According to the Mayo Clinic website, exercise controls weight, combats health conditions and diseases, improves mood, boosts energy, and promotes better sleep. Even taking a 20- or 30-minute walk does something beneficial for the body.

6. *Spend some time in nature.* A stroll through a tree-lined trail or hiking in hills and mountains is a great way to reduce stress, lift your spirits, and improve your fitness.
7. *Turn off the TV and pick up a good book.* Reading is relaxing—and educational.

In conclusion, your habits, your attitudes, and the activities you are involved in all have a direct impact on your energy level.

Joe's Recap

Habits and Getting Free

- Good habits make us more effective and productive. If you really want to change your life, start by changing your habits.
- Adopting a new routine and staying with it helps a new habit become ingrained. Good habits free up our mind to concentrate on other activities.
- If you need to lose weight and make a health turnaround, then don't delay one day. Start with a time of reflection, and make a plan to do something about your health.
- You will have more opportunities to learn something that could be useful to you and to your career if you're not solely focused on entertaining yourself with watching TV and online videos while participating in social media.
- Speaking ill of others is a ruinous habit because it creates negative energy. What you say almost always gets back to the person you're talking about.
- Before saying something not very nice, step back and ask yourself these three questions:
  - Is it good?
  - Is it useful?
  - Is it truthful?
    If you can't say yes to all three, then don't say it.

- Before you go to bed, take 10 minutes to reflect or read something inspirational or uplifting, or you can write in a journal the answers to the following questions:
  1. What was the best thing that happened today?
  2. What am I most grateful for today?
  3. What did I do to live my ideal day today?
  4. What is one new thing I learned today?
  5. What did I do to meet my goals today?
  6. What am I most looking forward to tomorrow?
- Instead of getting up in the morning and checking your e-mail, settle into the day by taking anywhere from 2 to 20 minutes being quiet, either reading or reflecting.
- Don't forget to drink lots of water, get at least 7 hours of sleep, eat healthy and avoid processed foods, limit alcohol, stay away from sodas, and exercise at least 20 minutes every day, even if it's just a walk around the neighborhood.

Exercises

1. What are some of your bad habits?

  _____

  _____

  _____

2. What effects do these bad habits have on your life, career, and relationships?

  _____

  _____

  _____

3. What's one bad habit you need to drop and replace with a healthy habit?

  _____

  _____

  _____

(continued)

(continued)

4. How much time do you spend on unimportant tasks each week?

_____

_____

_____

5. What are some productive activities or projects you could better spend this time on?

_____

_____

_____

6. How much of your life do you dedicate to education and learning versus entertainment? What is your actual ratio of hours per week spent on entertainment compared with the number of hours per week spent on education?

_____

_____

_____

CHAPTER **11**

Get Free with Energizing People and Activities

Get Free

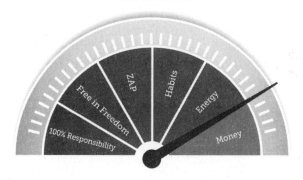

You are the average of the five people you spend the most time with.

—JIM ROHN, author of *My Philosophy for Successful Living*

Having positive, healthy habits can greatly contribute to our success, but so can spending time with certain people in our lives. The people we spend time with, the activities we are involved in, and the events we attend can make us more productive, effective, and motivated—or they might not if we choose poorly.

Surrounding ourselves with people who are supportive, inspiring, and encouraging is key to living a more productive and meaningful life. You might want to ask yourself: *Whom am I hanging out with? How are those people influencing my thoughts and behaviors?*

Many of the thoughts we carry around with us come from the past—from parents, family members, teachers, bosses, or pastors. Even if these people are no longer associated with your life— either because you've moved on or they've passed away—they said things that became deeply embedded within you.

Take some time during the year to reflect on who energizes you and with whom you want to spend time in the coming year. The people you surround yourself with and the media you consume have a large impact on the quality of your life. Everyone likes being around people who think like us, not in the sense that we have to agree on everything but in the context that they share our view of the world. We see a similar big picture. At the same time, we can also learn from people who see the world differently from us.

On the day after Thanksgiving in 2012, I was thinking about the coming year. Who are the people that I get most energized from? Who are the people that, at the end of an evening, have me saying to myself, *why don't I spend more time with them?*

So when I began mapping out what I wanted to accomplish in the New Year, beyond setting financial goals and professional accomplishments I wanted to achieve, I also made note of the people I *wanted* to spend time with and whom I *needed* to spend time with, both personally and professionally.

The result transformed my life because in the past, I wasn't deliberate in choosing whom I spent my time with. If someone I knew asked me to join him or her at a chamber mixer held at the University of Wisconsin–Milwaukee to hear a panel talk about the local economy, I was apt to say yes. I never knew whether that could turn into a business opportunity.

But after this time of reflection after Thanksgiving, I made a new rule: *Spend as much time as possible with people who energize me.* That meant if certain energy drainers invited me to an event, I'd politely decline the invitation but accept an invitation if someone whose company I *did* enjoy asked me to join him or her at a similar function or social event.

You don't want to hang out with people who zap your energy. You want to surround yourself with those who invigorate you, ask good questions, tell great stories, and listen to what you have to say. You want to surround yourself with lifelong learners. These folks make events more enjoyable rather than something to be dreaded.

How do you feel about people who drain your energy, in whose presence you can feel your enthusiasm wane?

When I drew up my latest list of people who energized me the most, the results inspired me. My list comprised people who had a positive personality as well as an attitude of gratitude.

Topping my list was Sister Camille Kliebhan, a Catholic nun who is the most peaceful, grace-filled, grateful, caring, and fun person I've ever met. She asks inquisitive questions. She listens thoughtfully to what people have to say and then makes follow-up inquiries that demonstrate she is listening closely. She loves to hear a good joke as well as share one. She's also 90 years old—but has a youthful spirit. (You'll learn more about Sister Camille in my final chapter.)

There was also Suzy Dickens, an 85-year-old widow who's an incredible storyteller. She's the mother of John Dickens, one of my good friends. Her late husband, John Sr., was on the board of the Green Bay Packers for 46 years, so Suzy and I share stories of our favorite memories of the Packers.

I wrote down Matt Smith's name, too. Matt owns SalesSmith, which produces logoed merchandise and apparel. Matt is one of the neatest, friendliest, and kindest men I know, married to a wonderful woman named Mary Caye, who's just as much fun to be around. Every time my wife and I say good-bye to this couple, I think, *How come we don't hang out more often?*

My list is peppered with people with personality, but I also have three young kids on my list: J. J., Jet, and Jonah, who live across the street. They are bursting with energy and are filled with love for my golden lab, Murph, and me. Many nights when I drive into my driveway, they come running over, give me a big hug, and pet Murph.

Because of them, I believe *you'll never go wrong making friends with people over 80 and kids under eight.* The wisdom of my senior friends and the innocence and youthful curiosity of children energize me and give me well-rounded perspective.

So, who energizes you? Can you list several people you look forward to seeing every time you get together? We all need friends who provide support, listen to our goals and desires, and are willing to share their insights.

Similarly, being a source of inspiration, motivation, and comfort for others will play an important role in keeping those special people in your life.

Seek, and You Shall Find

What should you do if you have no option but to spend a part of your day with energy-draining people and activities?

First, continuing to be your best self, leading by example, and being a positive force can inspire others to also be more positive. Next, be proactive in bringing energizing people to you and meeting up with like-minded people. Make lunch appointments with friends you enjoy spending time with. It doesn't have to be lunch; it could be something as simple as going for a walk, working out together, or grabbing a cup of coffee.

As for meeting more people who energize you, identify what your interests are and how you can meet more people who share these interests. If you're a skier or a knitter, you'll be able to find associations that share your interests.

THE RULE OF THREE

To increase the odds of surrounding yourself with those who can keep you engaged and lift your spirits, consider employing the *Rule of Three*.

First, there are the people you can spend 3 minutes with and be okay. Let's face it: We should be able to do that with everyone, even the town crank or politicians from the other side of the aisle.

Of course, there are some people that we just don't gel with, but that's okay. But for the vast majority of people, 3 minutes is no problem.

Next are the people you could spend *3 hours* with. Basically, that means their presence energizes you. You have common ground, can partake in give-and-take conversation, and remain engaged. You would thoroughly enjoy a 3-hour dinner with these people.

The final category is the people you could spend *three days* with and have as much fun on the third day as you were having on the first. These would be your good friends, close colleagues, golf buddies, or travel companions.

Are you spending your precious time with people who free you up as well as energize you? Do you find you spend too many 3-day weekends with 3-minute people? These are significant questions because people can be key to discovering our energy and freedom.

TAKING A LOOK AROUND

When you stop and think about it, there's a lot of energy around us from people, places, and events. So what energy are you creating in your environment?

Your mind-set also plays as big a role in how energetic you feel. If you have negative attitudes holding you down or holding you back, it's up to you—the one taking 100 percent responsibility—to do something about it. So part of getting free, of getting your habits in line, is asking yourself these questions:

- What gives you energy?
- Who gives you energy?
- What types of activities increase your energy?
- What types of activities drain your energy?

Energy-zapping activities include lengthy meetings that could have been finished in 15 minutes but are stretched to fill the allotted 90 minutes, thus proving true the old adage *work expands to fill the space*. Or you might work beside colleagues who are disruptive, unreasonable, or ineffective. Repetitive tasks and unproductive projects also tire the mind and the body.

Everyone faces challenges. Everyone has to overcome negativity and adversity on the road to success. Jon Gordon, author of *The Energy Bus,* adds that no one goes through life untested. The answer to these tests is to exude positive energy—the kind of positive energy that consists of the vision, optimism, enthusiasm, purpose, and spirit that defines great leaders and their dreams.

This series of questions will help you better understand where you fall and where you want to be:

1. *Where is your energy level on a scale of 1 to 10?*

    If 1 is no energy and 10 represents the energy of a young adult in the prime of his or her life, where do you fall? If you are at a 4, but you feel like you need an energy level at 8, you need to make changes that will increase your energy. In other words: You need to match your energy level with your desired outcomes.

> **A Sales Tip**
>
> If sales is part of your job description, then keep this thought in the back of your mind: People want to buy from people who have an energy level of 8, 9, or 10.

    Even if you feel your natural level is a 5, you can achieve a level of energy in the 7 to 9 range. The thing about energy that most people forget is the more you do, the more energy you feel. Many people fear exerting themselves—in the workplace, at home, or at the gym. They are sure that those efforts will deplete their energy stores and they'll have nothing left to give. Actually, the opposite happens; work delivers energy to the mind and the muscles.

2. *What do you want to accomplish in your day, during the week, or in the next year?*

If you're seeking the ideal life, then thinking things through and making plans are important first steps. Maybe you need a weekend planning retreat or need to attend a workshop or seminar to help you get clear. Once you come up with a plan, make sure that executing that plan is a part of your everyday ritual.

Because life can get busy, be sure to set reminders of what tasks lie ahead each day as they relate to your short-term and long-term goals. It's necessary to be striving for new goals and achievements consistently and not to let day-to-day tasks prevent you from working toward your larger goals.

3. *What energy level do you need to accomplish everything you want to do?*

Only you know your body best, so what level do you need to be at to get everything done that you set out to do today? One way to keep your energy level high is to work with people who share your drive and challenge you to be better.

4. *What is your energy gap?*

If you feel like you normally operate at 5 and want to be at 9, you have a gap of 4. Knowing where you are is helpful because awareness is often the first step toward addressing an issue.

5. *What habits are you going to create or eliminate to close the gap?*

Choose activities that give you energy. It could be going on a bike ride, playing a round of golf, learning new songs on the guitar, building a model train set, or even taking an unexpected nap in a backyard hammock. Don't feel guilty about taking a short time from your day to do something outside your normal routine.

Volunteering to help others or being part of a community organization, philanthropy, or school event can be some of the most energizing hours of your life. Volunteering has surprising benefits as well: You can make new friends, learn new skills, protect your mental and physical health, and even advance your career. Unpaid volunteers are often the glue that holds a community together, and you can be a part of that. Dedicating your time as a volunteer boosts your social skills and expands your network. Be sure to volunteer for an activity or an organization that you are passionate about.

Of course, you have to guard against overcommitting yourself to too many activities that take your free hours away from family and friends. If you feel you're overcommitted, then reflect—during those 10 minutes before you go to sleep or when you wake up—if those activities match your goals and priorities.

Joe's Recap

Get Free with Energizing People and Activities

- Getting free requires you to identify self-limiting thoughts and behaviors that are holding you back and then eliminate them. If you're not feeling free, you might want to ask yourself whom you are hanging out with or where your thoughts are coming from.
- Exercise forethought about the movies you watch, the books you read, the films you see, and the shows you watch on TV.
- Who energizes you? You want to hang out with people who invigorate you, ask good questions, tell great stories, and listen to what you have to say.
- Make a list of 10 people who energize you the most. When's the last time you saw some of these folks? Do you need to make plans to get in touch soon?
- You'll never go wrong making friends with people over 80 and kids under eight. The wisdom of our senior friends and the innocence and youthful curiosity of children will give you a better perspective on life.
- To increase the odds of surrounding yourself with those who can keep you animated and lift your spirits, you

should employ the *Rule of Three*. Although there are people we can spend 3 minutes with, you want to gravitate toward friends and acquaintances with whom you'd love to spend 3 hours or 3 days.

Exercises

1. List several people who energize you. What about them has you looking forward to spending a meal or a weekend with them?

_____

_____

_____

2. Who are the five people that you spend the most time with? Are they energizers or energy drainers?
Professional:

1. _____

2. _____

3. _____

4. _____

5. _____

Personal:

1. _____

2. _____

3. _____

4. _____

5. _____

3. List three types of activities that give you energy. What types of activities drain your energy?

_____

_____

_____

(continued)

(*continued*)

4. List three types of events that give you energy. Which kinds of events drain you of energy?

_____

_____

_____

5. List three places that give you energy. What places drain your energy?

_____

_____

_____

6. How would you describe your energy level on a scale of 1 to 10? What energy level do you need to accomplish your goals? What is the gap? What can you do to close the gap?

_____

_____

_____

7. When is your energy level the highest: in the morning hours, midway through the day, or into the evening hours?

_____

_____

_____

8. What do you want to accomplish this week? List and prioritize. (Examples: work 45 hours, see two of my kids' soccer games, or visit ill parents.)

_____

_____

_____

CHAPTER **12**

Get Free with Your Money

Get Free

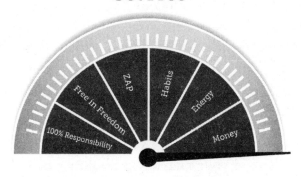

We buy things we don't need with money we don't
have to impress people we don't like.

—DAVE RAMSEY, author of *The Total Money Makeover:
A Proven Plan for Financial Fitness*[1]

One time, a parish finance director called a wealthy parishioner.

"Our records show that you are a millionaire and that you have
not contributed any money to the church. We need a new roof.
Can you help us?"

The rich tycoon fired back, "Do your records show that I have a
95-year-old mother with enormous medical bills? Do your records
show that I have a sister whose husband deserted her, leaving her
seven children to raise on her own? Do your records show that I
have a blind and incapacitated nephew who needs my help?"

The parish finance director immediately backpedaled. "I'm so
sorry," he said. "Our records don't show any of those things. On
behalf of the church, we are so sorry."

"That's okay," the wealthy parishioner responded. "If I didn't help any of them, why would I give the church any money?"

Of all the places where people are least likely to be free, it's in the area of finances. Because money can play a big role in why people don't feel free, it's imperative to figure out how much is enough. So, how much is enough? It's my estimation that it's usually 10 percent more than what we have—meaning that most of us are never satisfied in the area of our finances.

I'm all for managing money well and financial planning. I've read plenty of books over the years about the virtues of spending less than you make, eating a sack lunch, and investing $6.25 a day for 45 years at 8 percent interest to retire with a million bucks in the bank. I also understand how difficult it is to keep the bills paid or put anything aside for retirement, but that's not what this chapter is all about.

I believe money can set you free in myriad ways if you change the way you look at your finances. I've always believed that one of the important purposes of money is to express appreciation and gratitude. Random acts of monetary kindness often have a way of coming back to you in ways you never expected.

In this mind-set, you don't *spend* money. You merely recirculate it. But for some, money and wealth have a set point, meaning that some people can't envision themselves making more than a certain amount of money, so the choices they make leave them always at the same level of income or debt.

You see it with lottery winners. The National Endowment for Financial Education estimates that as many as 70 percent of lottery winners squander their winnings and end up bankrupt and divorced as well as bereft of family and friends because sudden wealth destroyed those relationships. Besides having little or no experience handling large sums of money, lottery winners also go bankrupt because deep down they don't feel like they deserved the unexpected windfall. They know they did nothing to earn the large check with six or seven zeros.

I saw this way of thinking as a sports agent in the 1990s. When people asked me this question—*Why do professional athletes go broke within a few years of retiring?*—I replied that they didn't feel like they deserved all those hundreds of thousands or millions of dollars that were showered on them during their brief professional careers. There's a reason why the National Football League (NFL) is also called the Not for Long league, and it's because careers usually last three or four years. Then the big paychecks stop overnight.

I'm convinced it's a mind-set issue. I knew one player who came out of the projects and grew up thinking that the most he could aspire to was becoming a drug dealer and making $50,000 a year. So when he made $1.2 million a year, he didn't think he deserved the money. Anything more than $50,000 was like gravy to him.

Then there are those who think that financial security is having enough money in the bank, but real security is the ability to handle what life gives you. Many people are living paycheck to paycheck and bracing for the next calamity. Thus, the pressure to live within our means can place tremendous stresses on us. It's hard to feel free under these circumstances.

Most people fall into four categories when it comes to their perspectives about money:

1. *A mind-set of scarcity:* Individuals with this frame of mind often feel like there's never enough to go around in their business, in their family, and in our economy. Everyone is scrambling for his or her piece of a finite pie.
2. *A mind-set of security:* Individuals with this frame of mind tend to feel like they have enough money to live on and can typically pay their bills. They are risk averse and prefer to maintain the status quo.
3. *A mind-set of success:* Individuals with this frame of mind typically have more than enough money, but they worry about their investments and retirement accounts. They have enough experience to know that nothing is guaranteed.
4. *A mind-set of abundance:* Individuals with this frame of mind realize there's more than enough for everybody. They don't see the economic pie as a zero-sum game. They see the world as a place of abundance where there's enough for everyone.

If you have a mind-set of scarcity, I encourage you to work toward a mind-set of abundance. One of the ways I do that for myself is leaving a few dollars behind at the cash register whenever I get my morning coffee at Sendik's Food Market, which I described in Chapter 4. I've seen how using money to bestow something unexpected on someone—such as a simple cup of coffee—keeps me in the right frame of mind regarding money.

Whether it's buying a fast-food meal for the soldier in uniform standing behind you or handing a grocery gift card to a single parent with two toddlers in tow, acting out of a mind-set of abundance will give your life meaning as well as a proper mind-set about money.

Worth Pondering on Walden Pond

The cost of a thing is the amount of what I will call life which is required to be exchanged for it.
—Henry David Thoreau, nineteenth-century author and philosopher in *Walden*

The Best Things in Life Are Free—Or Almost Free

List the 10 things you enjoy most in life. How many of them would cost little or no money? Here are a few ideas:

- Walking on the beach or in a park with your dog
- Sitting with kids or friends in front of a crackling fire
- Reading a good book
- Going for a run or a long walk
- Preparing a meal for the kids or grandkids
- Playing the guitar (or your favorite musical instrument)
- Watching the sun set with your spouse or partner
- Having friends over for a barbecue
- Watching football on a Saturday or Sunday afternoon
- Taking an afternoon nap

DEALING WITH DEBT

Many people these days have taken on too much debt, which causes them to operate with a scarcity mind-set. Start dealing with debt by being more conscious about your spending. The fact is that money is one of the most important elements in our lives—especially when you don't have enough. When the month's expenses exceed the income, the stress can be paralyzing. Your ability to move about freely is severely compromised when you're deep in debt.

I've been in debt many times, especially early in my marriage when I was attending Notre Dame to earn my MBA. Tami and I were surprised to find out she was pregnant. We didn't have health insurance to cover the blessed event of our son's birth, which cost $3,000. Then six months later, we learned she was pregnant again—but we didn't have health insurance because I was a few months away from finishing my MBA and getting my first full-time job with full health care benefits. Our second son's birth roughly cost $3,500.

After I graduated from Notre Dame, I had $50,000 in student debt and $6,500 in hospital debt. I knew I had to establish a plan that involved making monthly payments that we could afford and that would allow us to live within our means. I figured it would take me 10 years to pay off all three debts.

Here's what I learned from my experiences: When you establish a payment plan and commit to it—even if angst and self-doubt creep in—you can say to yourself, "I have a plan."

Financial counselors, such as Dave Ramsey, host of a national radio show on financial matters, recommend that you pay off your smallest debt first instead of the debt with the highest interest. He says this *debt snowball* plan gives you some quick wins to stay pumped enough to get out of debt completely. When you start knocking off the smaller debts, the results embolden you, and debt reduction snowballs from there.

Every time you pay off a debt, "you can see how close you are getting to freedom," Ramsey says.[1]

Got Clutter?

Clutter around your place of work or your home isn't freeing at all. Cleaning the spaces around you has a way of clearing the mind, so do the three Ds: declutter, dehoard, or donate. Cleaning out files, carrying filled cardboard boxes to the recycling bin, sprucing up your workspace, and giving away reusable items to a local charity can help you feel freer.

If you tend to leave stuff around and allow piles to rise, take a couple of hours to get free. A cleaned-up work area lifts your spirits and keeps you better focused.

CREDIT CARDS: A FORM OF MODERN-DAY SLAVERY

We've become a cashless society where pretty much everything is paid for with the swipe of a credit card or debit card. We can even point our smartphones at a financial reader and be done with our purchase.

Paying with a credit card or smartphone gives you the feeling that you have money anytime you want—even when you really don't have money. When you don't pay the outstanding balance in full every month—or you overdraw your checking account—that can really add up in interest and bank charges. Most credit cards charge 1.5 percent interest per month or 18 percent interest annually, so if you have a $5,000 balance that you need to pay off, that comes to at least $900 annually or $75 a month—on interest alone! Also, many credit cards levy more usurious rates of 21 percent or even 27 percent annually, depending on your credit score.

So if you truly want to get free from credit card debt, consider these strategies:

1. *Get your credit cards paid off.* If you have outstanding credit card debt, you're going to have to work overtime or take a second job.

2. *Put a freeze on credit card spending.* Use cash or checks to pay for your food, gas, entertainment incidentals, and various bills. That way you can spend only the money that's in your bank account, which acts as a governor of your spending. You'll have to be far more disciplined and track how much is going out as well as what's coming in.

3. *Stick to the plan.* The plan is paying down those credit cards. As mentioned before, send the largest payment possible to the credit card with the smallest amount of debt. That way, you witness—and enjoy—the progress you're making. When that debt is paid off, pay extra toward the next biggest debt. Do the same until all your credit cards are paid off.

4. *If you continue to use credit cards, then use only one.* It's just a lot easier to track your spending if you use only one card.

The $2 Bill

I still like cash. When I'm in a restaurant and paying with a credit card, I'll tip the waitress or waiter with $2 bills.

You should see their eyes light up! Two-dollar bills are such a rarity these days that I hear many recipients say they are lucky. I'm just trying to give them a unique experience— and show them that cash still makes an impression.

A NEW WAY OF LOOKING AT MONEY

It's natural to be concerned about living within one's means.

Try to do the following things:

1. Explore your thinking and mind-set about money.
2. Before purchasing something, ask yourself, "Do I really need this?"
3. When you *do* spend money, see yourself as recirculating money.

4. To get a handle on your expenses, record your purchases on software, such as Quicken, so that you can keep track of everything you spend.
5. Don't be afraid to ask for help.

This chapter is about changing your mind-set and the way you look at money. If you can see that we live in a world of abundance versus a world of lack, you'll always have more than enough.

Money and finances are more than what you are lacking. It's important to understand how much is enough in your life and have the discipline to live within your means.

Joe's Recap

Get Free with Your Money

- People generally fall into one of four categories when it comes to money:
  1. *A mind-set of scarcity:* Individuals with this frame of mind often feel like there's never enough to go around.
  2. *A mind-set of security:* Individuals with this frame of mind tend to feel like they have enough money to live on and can typically pay their bills.
  3. *A mind-set of success:* Individuals with this frame of mind typically have more than enough money, but they worry about their investments and retirement accounts.
  4. *A mind-set of abundance:* Individuals with this frame of mind realize there's more than enough for everybody. They see the world as a place of abundance where there's more than enough for everyone.
- People with a scarcity of money mind-set can improve a situation by reframing how they think about money.

- The solution in many households is to run up credit card debt, which becomes a form of modern-day slavery.
- Many financial counselors recommend that you pay off your smallest debt first instead of the debt with the highest interest. Knocking out even small debts can motivate you to get all your debt down to zero.
- Check out www.becomingminimalist.com as a tool to help you get free with money.

Exercises

1. Where are you on the money mind-set category? What changes can you make to begin moving from scarcity to security to success to abundance?

_____

_____

_____

2. When's the last time you took a firm look at your finances? Do you need to come up with a plan to help you reach your financial goals?

_____

_____

_____

3. Describe in detail how much is enough.

_____

_____

_____

4. Determine your needs and your wants as well as how much discretionary income you need. How much do you really have available to spend each month?

_____

_____

_____

(continued)

(continued)

5. Study how economics should be affecting your spending. Do you recalculate your fixed costs as gas prices go up and adjust your discretionary income accordingly?

_____

_____

_____

6. In terms of housing, are you buying or renting only what you need? Think about this as well as all the additional expenses included in the purchase. Ask yourself honestly whether this home will bring freedom or place a burden on your life. Repeat this exercise with the cars you drive, the technology you use, and the major purchases you make.

_____

_____

_____

SECTION

Get Going

In this final section of *Moving the Needle,* we will explore some of the best business practices that can really move the needle for you and your career.

We all need to develop systems and put them into practice to get going in life. No one wants to stay in the same place personally or in a career. Everyone likes making steady progress toward goals that further ourselves.

So, let me ask you this: What's motivating you? Where are you spending your time and putting your focus? Are you inspired? The reason I ask that last question is because most people don't do anything until they're inspired, but once they are, there's almost nothing they won't do.

The following five best practices can keep you inspired every day you show up for work. In the following chapters, you will learn how to:

- Stay accountable for what you want to accomplish each day.
- Surround yourself with trusted advisors who have your back.
- Expand your network by finding bird dogs.
- Think outside the box through *mindstorming*.
- Differentiate yourself by using something I call the Sweeney 22.

These practices or systems will assist you in moving the needle and give you higher levels of satisfaction at work and at home. Once you get going, you can take your game to the next level by checking out my 52-Week Winning Game Plan for Business and Personal Development. You can find out more about the 52-Week Game Plan, which can be tailored to an 8-, 16-, or 52-week program based on your needs, by flipping to the back of this book.

CHAPTER **13**

The 5/10/15 Plan

Get Going

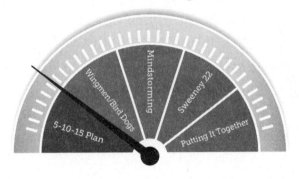

There is always one more thing you can do to increase
your odds of success.

—Hal Moore, U.S. Army lieutenant general, retired

Systems are good because they create good habits, and good
habits create or change behaviors. To help me stay connected,
keep myself accountable to my job and my superiors, and develop
new prospects and clients, I've created a system called the 5/10/15
plan (Figure 13.1).

My system will help you become accountable to yourself.
Accountability is a matter of living on principle, showing honesty
and integrity to work hard, and being responsible for your actions
and your decisions. The 5/10/15 plan is an important tool to get
you going in the right direction. You may not have thought about
the need for a personal accountability system, but the 5/10/15 plan
gives you a great road map for each workday.

The 5/10/15 Plan	
5 meetings/encounters (daily)	**What's in it for *them*?**
1.	
2.	
3.	
4.	
5.	
10 correspondences (daily)	
1.	
2.	
3.	
4.	
5.	
6.	
7.	
8.	
9.	
10.	
15 phone calls (daily)	
1.	
2.	
3.	
4.	
5.	
6.	
7.	
8.	
9.	
10.	
11.	
12.	
13.	
14.	
15.	

FIGURE 13.1   The 5/10/15

Here's a quick explanation of how the 5/10/15 plan works:

- The 5 means that you try to have five meetings or encounters a day. A meeting or encounter moves your agenda forward or gets you closer to your goal or desired outcome. A meeting doesn't mean sitting down in a conference room with eight colleagues at 9 AM or going out to lunch for 90 minutes. A meeting means making some sort of contact with a person, even if it means you're both standing in line at a coffee shop.
- The 10 means that you send out 10 letters or pieces of correspondence, mainly on corporate stationery, every day. Personal e-mails can count in this area but not impersonal e-blasts.
- The 15 means that you make a minimum of 15 phone calls a day. The most important part of the call is to ask at the end, "Is there anything I can do for you or your family?" because we are all in business to serve others and show we truly care. It is imperative to think about what's in it for them as well as yourself.

The best part about the 5/10/15 plan is the accountability it brings to you and those in your life. Accountability is the acknowledgment of responsibility for your actions and your decisions. Accountability is a matter of taking 100 percent responsibility, being true to yourself, and having the honesty and integrity to do the right thing when no one else is looking.

If you're looking for a system that reinforces personal accountability, let the 5/10/15 plan work for you. This focused and disciplined approach will keep you in the game, help you stay on track, grow your business, and give you a sense of accomplishment.

THE VALUE OF A GREAT SYSTEM

You may not have thought about the need for a personal accountability system, but the 5/10/15 plan gives you a system for success.

If you think about it, systems are everywhere in the business world. McDonald's is a leading example. McDonald's may not have the best hamburgers, but it has the best system in the fast-food business, in my opinion. The McDonald's way of doing things begins with the way it prepares its food, which is why a Big Mac in Milwaukee is the same as a Big Mac in Miami. That's product consistency.

Whatever business you're in, you're probably looking for consistency as well. The 5/10/15 plan is all about consistency and will help you help you network and connect with people better in the workplace. The best part of the 5/10/15 plan is the way the system promotes connections, which ultimately help you deepen your relationships. That's significant because *when you meet someone face to face, it's easier to see eye to eye.*

If you've ever asked yourself on a Friday afternoon, "What did I get done this week?" then the 5/10/15 program will give you an answer because this system helps you document all your meetings, phone calls, and correspondence you made during the workweek. They're all there in black and white. There's no place to hide.

> **Worth Repeating**
>
> When you meet face to face, it's easier to see eye to eye.
>
> —Joe Sweeney

The 5/10/15 plan can also be adapted and used in areas of your life beyond your career. You can employ this system of personal accountability for a job search. For instance, how many human resources (HR) departments or possible job contacts did you reach out to today—or this week—to land a job? Did you broaden your base of contacts by keeping track of e-mails or correspondence you sent out? You'll know because you wrote down or kept track of your phone calls, meetings, and the e-mails you sent out.

MAKING THE RIGHT CONNECTIONS

Why is the 5/10/15 plan important? Or perhaps the better question would be: Why does the 5/10/15 plan work so well?

When it comes to growing your business, connecting with your prospects and clients on a deeper level, and expanding your network, the 5/10/15 plan provides a template and a system to implement in your daily work. The 5/10/15 plan fosters relationships, which are the foundation of building business for you and your company. It's all about making the connections.

As for sending out 10 pieces of correspondence, this may be as simple as printing out a story online or clipping a newspaper article, attaching your business card, and putting everything in an envelope to mail. This part of the plan usually takes no more than 15 minutes each morning.

What about texting? Texts can comprise a part of your 5/10/15 plan as long as the majority of the communications are thoughtful and deliberate. With texting, I have a standing rule: If I receive two unclear texts (or e-mails) on the same topic or subject matter, and I still don't understand what's going on, I call that person.

Look at the 5/10/15 plan as a focused and disciplined system that will help you grow your business and give you a sense of accomplishment. Business has been and always will be about connecting with people. When interpersonal connections are made, you'll feel like you're getting somewhere.

THE PLAN

To stay on track with the 5/10/15 plan, you can type in your entries for meetings, phone calls, and records of correspondence into a spreadsheet, or print out five copies of the 5/10/15 plan and place them in a three-ring binder, one for each day of the workweek, Monday through Friday. Remember, with each encounter, keep in mind what's in it for the other person.

Here's the best way to use this system:

1. *Begin by taking 20 minutes on Sunday night to map out your week.* I mentioned earlier how you can plan your week using the food, daily exercise, and adequate water (FEW) plan and reviewing your Life Decision Wheels. On Sunday

night, review your appointments, schedule exercise times, review the meetings you have to prepare for, and analyze your commitments for the coming week. If you do some planning and review on Sunday night, you'll feel much more prepared when you wake up on Monday morning.

2. *When you arrive at your desk, sync your 5/10/15 program with any meetings or engagements you're planning for that day.* You'll feel great checking them off and getting a good start to the morning.

3. *It's okay to have a loose definition for a* meeting. Whenever I run into a business contact while picking up my morning coffee, that hi-how-ya-doing exchange could qualify as a meeting if it moves your goals or objectives forward. Why? Because you had face time and made a connection.

4. *In this age, making and receiving phone calls is a piece of cake.* If you have a smartphone, it's easy to make phone calls or do callbacks when you're out.

5. *The most critical thing to say at the end of a phone call to show that you truly care is this:* "If there is anything I can do for you or your family, please let me know."

6. *Don't rely on e-mail for all your correspondence.* I know that we're supposed to be working in a paperless environment, but I still send out handwritten notes marking a birthday or some achievement in that person's life or his or her children's lives. There's something about the personal touch that deepens the connection.

7. *Find something nice to say in your handwritten letters.* What should you write about when you send a personal note through the mail? I usually play off something I saw in the newspaper or an article posted online. For instance, if there is a contact I've done business with in the past, and I see his kid made the all-star team, I'll clip the story from the newspaper or print out the online story. Then I'll underline the child's name with a yellow highlighter and tuck the clipping along with a personal note congratulating

the parent and the family into the envelope. The key to the handwritten notes is to find something personal and do something memorable.

8. *Be in it for the long haul.* Using the 5/10/15 program isn't easy at the beginning, but stay with it. New habits become ingrained with repetition, so it will take a conscious effort to adopt a different way of doing things.

GET GOING ON BUILDING YOUR CLIENT BASE

The 5/10/15 plan takes discipline to execute, but as they say in golf, the more you practice, the more efficient you get.

Sure, building your business and your career takes skill and a certain amount of good fortune, but it's also a numbers game. In a numbers game, you just can't talk about doing something. You have to *get going* if you're going to make things happen.

How do you do it? By taking things one step at a time—one meeting, one letter, and one phone call at a time. Sure, that first phone call, first letter, or first meeting is daunting. By now, you may be saying to yourself, "That's way too much, Joe. This is over the top for me."

If the 5/10/15 plan seems overwhelming, back off and try a 3/6/9 or a 2/4/6 program. You've got to start somewhere and create some sort of accountability system to spur you on. Once you get going, the results will surprise you. Even an abbreviated approach—such as three meetings, six correspondences, and nine calls daily—will take you a lot further down the road than doing nothing. Ditto for two meetings, four correspondences, and six phone calls. But even if that sounds too formidable to you, then try to write three handwritten notes a day for five days. That will be 15 handwritten notes in a week, which creates some impetus.

Keep the long-term goal in mind. When you implement the 5/10/15 plan wholeheartedly, that means 30 contact points per day,

600 per month, and 7,200 per year. After 30 years, that's more than 216,000 connections.

What other system could take you that far?

THE PERSONAL TOUCH NEVER GOES OUT OF STYLE

Besides helping you in your business career, the 5/10/15 program can help you differentiate yourself and become known as the *person who still writes handwritten notes*.

Sure, you have to have some decent stationery on hand and pay for postage, but sending a letter in the mail still means a great deal and counts more than sending an e-mail message.

During the first year *Networking Is a Contact Sport* was on bookshelves, I received hundreds of e-mails from people congratulating me for writing a fine book or saying how much they enjoyed learning that networking was a place you go to give, not to get.

To be honest, I can't remember many of those e-mails today.

But I also received numerous heartfelt, handwritten notes from people saying the same thing, and I saved every one of them. On occasion, I will still pull them out and read them. There's something about holding a letter, written on personal stationery in someone's own handwriting—or typed—that reveals personality as well as passion. Seeing someone's words and reading his or her thoughts make a far more indelible impression and lasts far longer than staring at a computer screen and reading a pixelized message. Sure, many times the words are the same, but there's something about the personal touch that has staying power.

If there is something you can write about and send to a colleague, potential business client, a casual acquaintance you want to know better, or a good friend who's had your back for a long time, don't procrastinate. Write that letter and mail it today.

So, whether you're looking for a job, wanting to increase your number of clients, hoping to become more accountable, or desiring to keep track of what you did in the past week, use the 5/10/15 plan to help you get going on fulfilling your goals.

Joe's Recap

The 5/10/15 Plan

To help you stay organized as well as focused in your personal life as well as your professional life, follow the 5/10/15 plan. Here are the basics of this system:

- The 5 refers to having five meetings or encounters a day. A meeting or encounter creates a connection, moves your agenda forward, or gets you closer to your goal or desired outcome.
- The 10 refers to sending out 10 letters or pieces of correspondence, mainly on corporate stationery, every day. Personal e-mails can count in this area but not impersonal e-blasts.
- The 15 refers to making a minimum of 15 phone calls a day. Many people in business have no problem fulfilling this directive.
- The 5/10/15 plan is a system that works because the calls and letters help make connections that can lead to face-to-face meetings. When you meet face to face, it's easier to see eye to eye.
- The most critical thing to say at the end of a phone call is, "If there is anything I can do for you and your family, please let me know." We're all in business to serve others, no matter what we do for a living.
- Don't forget the value of a handwritten note.
- Be known as the person who returns phone calls and answers e-mails. You don't want the reputation of someone who ignores people who try to get in touch with you.

Exercises

1. To get started on the 5/10/15 plan, create five copies of the 5/10/15 plan for the week ahead. Make a list of

(continued)

(*continued*)

10 potential prospects. Focus on working these names into your 5/10/15 this week (Figure 13.1).

1. _____
2. _____
3. _____
4. _____
5. _____
6. _____
7. _____
8. _____
9. _____
10. _____

2. Now list five prospects who became clients at one time or another. What did you do to move them from prospects to clients?

1. _____
2. _____
3. _____
4. _____
5. _____

3. Who are your best clients?

1. _____
2. _____
3. _____
4. _____
5. _____

4. What makes them your best clients? When's the last time you contacted each of these clients?

1. _____
2. _____
3. _____

4. _____

5. _____

5. If you work for a company, who are the top three producers? List them. Why are they so successful? What are their habits and communication skills?

    1. _____

    2. _____

    3. _____

6. Analyze your markets, prospects, and ideal clients. Whom could you ask to help you connect with them? What is your value proposition?

_____

_____

_____

CHAPTER **14**

Wingmen and Bird Dogs

Get Going

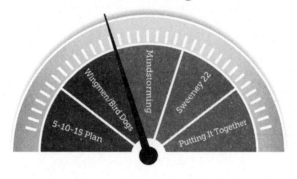

The only easy day was yesterday.

—Motto of the U.S. Navy SEALs

As you do the work of moving toward your goals, it can be helpful to secure the support of people around you to help keep you motivated and progressing in the right direction.

Too often we keep mention of our plans, our goals, and any obstacles in our way out of our conversations. We don't want to open ourselves to questions or criticism. For these reasons and more, we don't discuss the things most important to us.

If you prefer not to talk about what you want to accomplish and what's in the way, try making those topics a part of conversations with close friends and colleagues anyway. The more people you engage in the conversation, the better the counsel you'll receive. Having a team whom you can count on to be a source of advice, counsel, encouragement, and motivation—I call them wingmen

FIGURE 14.1   Do you have wingmen or wingwomen to watch your back?

or wingwomen—can make short work of tasks and decisions that otherwise seem daunting.

The term *wingmen* is military in origin. According to U.S. Air Force doctrine, a pair of fighter jets always flies in formation with one aircraft out in front and the other flying off the lead pilot's right wing and slightly behind. The second pilot is called the *wingman* and is given the charge to watch the lead pilot's back.

Back on the ground, wingmen are the people you'd choose if you were putting together a personal board of directors. They act as sounding boards. They're available to talk with you about what's happening in your life and what you're feeling. They are good listeners.

Top executives at large companies understand the value of having a board of directors who give them clarity and advice. In corporate terms, these members of the board are wingmen—the people looking out for you and who have your back. Wingmen are not only colleagues whom you can approach when you need outside-the-box advice, but they can also be encouragers in times of crisis. People need someone they can call on when they feel alone.

Wingmen know you and like you, and you can trust them to keep your conversations confidential. A wingman will pick you up when you fall down and tell you when the time is right to advance.

During the course of the past 25 years, I've asked people close to me to be my wingmen. My first wingman was my cousin Bob Sweeney, who took me under his wing when I was going through some major decisions with the sale of my first company. My cousin gave me clarity at a time when I wasn't able to see the path ahead.

Over the years, I added more wingmen when I explained to them what I was trying to do. I said I wanted them close to me so that they could help me avoid disasters, give me vision to see matters more clearly, encourage me to get out of my comfort zone when the situation warranted it, and stretch me in ways that I never thought possible.

These days I have a dozen wingmen. They are my go-to guys whom I meet with periodically, either all together in a small group or one on one. I encourage you to start building your personal board of directors by asking two or three close friends to become your wingmen. You will be pleasantly surprised by how these sounding boards can give you clarity and focus on matters large and small.

How often should you see each other? Most of the time, you'll want to meet every couple of months, perhaps over a lunch or dinner. That's where you can open up on what's happening in your life, both professionally and personally. They'll listen to you, discuss what your options are, and if they know they have the freedom to speak freely to you, point out why you need to go in a certain direction or what would be the best decision to make.

When it comes to getting going, creating your own personal board of directors can offer you an outside perspective on the problems and issues you confront. You want wingmen whom you can trust to keep your conversations confidential and your relationships on an even keel.

Having wingmen in your life will also deepen your friendships in ways you didn't think possible. If you've gone through your contact list, however, and really wonder whether you know anyone well enough whom you could approach, then I have an idea for you:

Ask anyway.

If you think you know someone who would make a good wingman, but you don't feel like you know him or her well enough to ask on the phone, then send an e-mail or a letter explaining what you're trying to do.

Here's what you can say when you ask someone about becoming your wingman:

Hi Ben:

I read this book called *Moving the Needle* by Joe Sweeney, and in the book, he talked about asking several people I know and respect to become a *wingman* for me. The term is military in origin and refers to a flight formation where there is a lead aircraft and two or more jets follow slightly behind and just off the wings of the lead pilot. These pilots flying behind the lead pilot are called wingmen because they've been given the charge to watch the lead pilot's back.

Because we have known each other socially and I respect all that you have done, I wanted to know whether you would be open to possibly becoming one of my wingmen. What this would mean is that I'd like to meet with you a few times a year and keep you up to date on what's happening in my business life as well as some personal areas of growth.

Thank you for your consideration and your willingness to meet with me to discuss my wingman idea.

To really get going in your career as well as your personal life, seek out wingmen who will encourage you, help you learn from your mistakes, and guide you to make the right decisions.

YOUR CIRCLE OF FRIENDS

Most people find the idea of having a personal board of close confidants in their lives very appealing. But in reality, we get busy at times, which makes it difficult to carve out time for even the most established relationships, let alone coordinate schedules to consult regularly with the new members of your board. Many people are finding out that it's their Facebook friends, Instagram followers, or LinkedIn connections they connect with the most.

But social media can take relationships only so far. I'm a believer in the truism that touch trumps technology. In today's social media universe, however, anyone can become your friend. My concern is that some people interact more with their electronic friends than with people in the flesh.

Your electronic friends are much different from the friends you could call on if you had a flat tire or needed someone to look after your kids if you had a family emergency. These are the friends in your community that you interact with regularly on a personal basis, someone you can grasp in a hug, tap on the shoulder, or shake hands in greeting.

Then there are your best friends—soul mates or confidants. These are close friends with whom you can share intimate details of your life because you've built up trust over the years. The assurance of friendship comes only after you have spent a great deal of time in each other's company—such as by sharing a pastime or hobby together or maybe several meals. The best definition of a great friend that I have heard is this: To be a great friend is to be the silent guardian of another person's solitude.

To get close with friends, you have to be open, honest, and comfortable with vulnerability. When you are vulnerable, it opens the door to intimacy. Intimacy builds deep trust.

Intimacy is everything when it comes to friends, so to help you determine who your intimate friends are, let me share a scale I introduced in *Networking Is a Contact Sport*. It's called the Friend Assessment Quotient, or FAQ. This 1-to-5 scale is a great tool in the business world as well as in social media. The purpose of this scale is to help you move the 1s, 2s, and 3s in your life into 4s and 5s.

What do these numbers mean? Here's an explanation:

- *1s are people you don't know.* With 317 million Americans and 7.1 billion people on this planet, you would be hard-pressed to say that you are really good friends with more than several hundred people.
- *2s are the people you barely know or know by name and not much else.* They can be people you'd like to get to know or who sound like they would be interesting to meet.
- *3s are your acquaintances, people you have met before and know well enough to say hello to.* These are people who might work in your department, or they are parents of your children's classmates or friends.
- *4s are your good friends, but this is actually a wide-open category.* These folks are your circle of friends. You like each other. You enjoy their company and spending time with them.
- *5s are your lifelines, your inner circle, and your wingmen.* The 5s are your closest friends, the ones you look to first for good advice and count on most for good counsel. They are the friends who'd be there for you because you'd be there for them.

How many 4s and 5s do you have? How many close friends could you call on if you had an emergency or life-changing event? When you open yourself up to developing deeper relationships, your friends will not only have your back but they also will give you clarity in life when you need it most.

If you're not able to touch base with your wingmen as often as you would like, try establishing a virtual board of directors for

Your Virtual Board of Directors

We all need role models. Although your personal board of directors is a great source of motivation and inspiration, it can be helpful to identify others you can draw strength from when you need it.

encouragement and motivation. I have pictures of 27 people in my planner who are my heroes and role models. Each one has traits I admire and want to emulate in my life.

Whenever I have challenging moments, I look to Abraham Lincoln for strength and guidance because of the adversity he overcame in his life. He lost congressional races, lost a Senate contest, lost a business, and went bankrupt. He had a complicated relationship with Mary Todd Lincoln and lost sons at the ages of 12 and four. He fought depression and nearly lost the Civil War, but he persevered. He exemplifies what it means to be resilient.

President Reagan was a great storyteller who used humor to overcome political divisiveness. Known as the Great Communicator, President Reagan possessed the unique ability to unite and inspire a nation in times of uncertainty. In my office, I have a picture of him with Speaker of the House Tip O'Neill. They were great adversaries who fought tooth and nail for what they believed in, but at the end of the day, they put their arms around each other and shared a beer and a few laughs. You don't see that happening any longer between the two political parties. President Reagan also reminds me of the importance of humor.

John Wooden won 10 National Collegiate Athletic Association (NCAA) basketball championships coaching for the University of California, Los Angeles, in the 1960s and early 1970s and could have been conceited for his accomplishments, and yet his number one trait was humility. Wooden famously said:

Talent is God-given. Be humble.

Fame is man-given. Be grateful.

Conceit is self-given. Be careful.

John Wooden is a constant reminder of the value of humility in our lives.

Many others are part of my virtual board: entrepreneurs, such as Henry Ford and Steve Jobs; great trainers, such as Jack Canfield and Wayne Dyer; former college football coach Lou Holtz, who's a master at humor and self-deprecation; and leaders, such as former

Green Bay Packers president Bob Harlan, who had an ability to connect deeply with and serve others.

I even have quotes from people who showed me how to grow old gracefully, such as comedians George Burns and Bob Hope, who both died coincidentally two months after celebrating their one hundredth birthdays. Sister Camille, who is a 91-year-old friend and Franciscan nun, provides spiritual inspiration. On the fitness side, Jack LaLanne's health and fitness practices and lifestyle are inspirational and stand the test of time.

Who are the historical figures, business leaders, authors, sports figures, or agents of change who inspire you? Begin collecting the quotes you come across that resonate with you and keep them somewhere where you can easily refer to them.

Your virtual board of directors will grow and change as you discover new sources of inspiration. The quotes and pictures you collect will remind you to live life better. If I need guidance for overcoming adversity, I'll read snippets and sayings from Abe Lincoln. If I need a reminder about what really counts, I'll repeat John Wooden's saying that I can't live a perfect day until I've done something for someone who can never repay me.

ROUND UP YOUR BIRD DOGS

There are wingmen, and there are bird dogs.

Bird dogs are different from your wingmen. Bird dogs are your eyes and ears outside the office, the ones who know what's happening in the marketplace and are able to communicate potential opportunities and help make connections for you.

Although wingmen can act as bird dogs for you, bird dogs are a more informal network of friends, business associates, and social contacts who can tell you what's going on in the community. They can be centers of influence (COIs): lawyers, accountants, and bankers. Whoever they are or whatever company or industry they come from, they can tip you off about prospective business deals going down, properties on the market, or people looking to hire or be hired.

Another way of looking at bird dogs is to view them as your scout team. They are aware of what's happening in the market-place and can give you *external* support, leads, and tips. On the other hand, *internal* support comes from your wingmen and wing-women, who offer listening ears and a wealth of valuable business experience.

One of my best bird dogs is a steel salesman who calls on around 250 manufacturing firms each year. He has his ear to the ground, which means he knows which companies are doing well, which ones are struggling, and which ones are on life support. When he tells me about companies that need to get sold, that is where the services of my investment banking firm can come in.

So, what about you? Do you have bird dogs out there looking for opportunities to grow your business? That's why it's imperative to set up a scout team that can bird-dog opportunities for you. If you embrace the philosophy that networking is a place you go to give, not to get, then you'll find that your bird dogs will be eager to bring you new leads and customers.

The best way to find bird dogs is to survey the marketplace and learn who's out there calling on your target businesses. Once you identify a bird dog, try to develop a relationship. Tell him or her who you are and what you do, and then let the relationship naturally develop. Over time, hopefully, you and your bird dog will like and trust each other. When he or she sends opportunities your way that result in business for you, then reciprocating will ensure that your relationship is a two-way street.

Cultivating bird dogs is a great way to connect with others, expand your network, and grow your business.

THE VALUE OF MENTORS

A mentor is someone who also acts as an advisor or a guide. Unlike a wingman, more often than not a mentor is someone who's older than you or more experienced.

One of my early mentors was the CEO of a large corpora-tion, a fellow named Tom. Tom and I were golfing one time. I was probably 30 years old, and he was in his mid-50s. We were sitting in the golf cart when he looked at me and said, "Whatever you do, Joe, make sure you spend time and raise your kids."

"Thanks, Tom. I appreciate the reminder. There are never enough hours in the day."

"You got that right. The biggest mistake I made was doing all that traveling, which really screwed things up at home because I wasn't there. If you think it's expensive and hard to raise kids, then try doing it when they are adults. I have several children, and many have had significant challenges in their lives."

Tom also talked to me about the value of creating a lifelong memory for each child every year. As a young father, I was all ears and filed away our conversation as a reminder not to spend too much time away from home. That was a real mentoring moment, even though Tom wasn't trying to advise me.

Today, more and more businesses understand the value of bringing in someone from the outside to mentor their CEOs or top leaders in a one-on-one coaching relationship. There's great value in having a mentor. Here are some ideas on how to find one:

- *Mentors are developed through networking*. Look for someone who is at a place in life where you want to be and has a wealth of experience. Figure out ways to network, connect, and build a relationship with this person.
- *Ask one of your senior wingmen if he or she would be willing to be more hands-on in coaching you*. If you have a close relationship, he or she will probably be thrilled to step into a mentoring role.
- *Seek out YouTube videos, podcasts, and blogs from well-known mentors*. I subscribe to numerous blogs and newsletters from inspiring and motivational people.
- *Read up on the topic*. Keeping current on the latest trends, changes, and theories in your industry is key not only to being successful, but also to establishing or maintaining a reputation for being on the leading edge of your industry. Identifying the thought leaders in your space and dedicating

the time to read their books, white papers, and articles will be invaluable to growing your business and adapting to an ever-changing marketplace.

- *Attend conferences, courses, and workshops.* Signing up for courses and workshops can provide opportunities to really dive deep into a subject. Also, a conference provides an opportunity to meet thought leaders in your industry.

You may not think you need a mentor, a wingman, a bird dog, or even more friends, but we all need input into our lives from people who've been there before. We can benefit from their advice as well as from hearing about the mistakes they have made.

Don't delay. You'll be glad you didn't delay because to get going, you need advisors and guidance that come from having wingmen, bird dogs, and mentors in your life, so reach out to someone today.

Joe's Recap

Wingmen and Bird Dogs

- Establishing and working with a strong support system made up of wingmen and bird dogs will help you get going.
- Wingmen are your sounding board and are available to talk with you about what's happening in your life and what you're feeling.
- A wingman will pick you up when you fall down and get in the foxhole with you when times get tough. A wingman will tell you to keep your head down until the offensive fusillade is over and when the time is right to advance.
- Ask two or three close friends or good friends to become your wingmen. These sounding boards can give you clarity and focus on matters large and small.
- The Friend Assessment Quotient, or FAQ, is a 1-to-5 scale that will help you determine who your friends are,

especially in the business world. The purpose is to help move the 1s, 2s, and 3s to 4s and 5s. Here is a breakdown:

- *1s are people you don't know.* These are all the people you haven't yet met.
- *2s are the people you know by name and not much else.* They can be people you'd like to get to know or who sound like they would be interesting to meet, either at work or where you congregate during your free time.
- *3s are your acquaintances, people you have met before and know well enough to say hello to.* You've chatted a few times but haven't established relationships with these people.
- *4s are your family and good friends.* Generally speaking, these folks are in your circle of friends. You have known each other for a period of time and enjoy each other's company.
- *5s are your lifelines, your inner circle, and your wingmen.* The 5s are your closest friends, the ones who play the biggest part in your day-to-day life and whom you'd call in the middle of the night if there were an emergency. They are the friends who'd be there for you no matter what.
- How many 5s do you have? How many close friends could you call on if you had an emergency? Your good friends not only have your back, but they will also always be there for you.
- You should also seek out bird dogs—a more informal network of friends, business associates, and social contacts who can be your eyes and ears in the community—and you can be the same for them.

(continued)

(continued)

- Bird dogs can inform you about prospective business opportunities, properties on the market, or people looking to hire or be hired.
- A mentor is someone who also acts as an advisor or a guide who can help you get clarity in your life from their wealth of life experiences.

Exercises

1. Do you have any wingmen? If you do, make a list of your wingmen.

_____

_____

_____

2. Why are these wingmen on your list? What are their strengths?

_____

_____

_____

3. If you don't have wingmen, whom could you ask? Why?

_____

_____

_____

4. How will you develop your relationship and stay accountable? Lunch once a week? A coffee break together?

_____

_____

_____

5. Do you have any bird dogs in your life? Whom could you ask?

_____

_____

_____

CHAPTER **15**

Mindstorming Ideas

Get Going

Just as your car runs smoothly and requires less
energy to go faster and farther when the wheels are
in perfect alignment, you perform better when your
thoughts, feelings, emotions, goals, and values are
in balance.

—BRIAN TRACY, author of *No Excuses! The Power of
Self-Discipline*[1]

One of the best tools to get going is a concept called *mindstorming,* a concept popular author and speaker Brian Tracy discusses frequently.

Tracy makes the analogy that building creative brainpower is a lot like building up your muscles in the gym: The more you exercise your ability to think creatively or find solutions to problems, the stronger your brain becomes. One of the best ways to pump "mental iron," he says, is to engage in a practice he calls mindstorming.

Mindstorming is a technique that facilitates the formulation of new or innovative ideas through a process that involves taking a question or conundrum and then brainstorming with others to provoke one of those aha! moments.

Mindstorming ... brainstorming. Aren't we talking about the same thing?

There are some subtle yet important differences. Brainstorming happens when we dedicate a set period to focusing on thinking about one topic or issue and considering all ideas that are generated in the hope of finding a creative solution. A productive brainstorm session promotes thinking outside the box. Brainstorming can take place as a group or individually.

Mindstorming takes brainstorming to the next level. Mindstorming begins by sitting down and writing a particular goal or problem at the top of the page. You must be as specific as you can. Then you embark on what Tracy calls the *20-Idea Method*, which means coming up with 20 solutions to a complex problem or difficult issue you're facing.

When doing the 20-Idea Method, the final few answers often contain your best solution, Tracy says. What happens is that you find yourself discarding the earlier—and more obvious—answers in favor of more creative ideas that often come toward the end. You must let your mind run to draw upon the fullness of your cerebral resources. American architect and inventor Buckminster Fuller said, "Your mind ultimately answers every question you ask it."

Let's take a typical problem for most people these days—earning more money, although I recognize that just hanging on to your job could be a bigger issue. But for the sake of argument, let's say that you would like to increase your salary from $50,000 a year to $75,000 a year in the next 12 months—an astonishing 50 percent increase.

So, at the top of the page, don't write, "How can I make some more money?" or "What can I do to increase my income by 50 percent?" Those questions are too generic. Instead, write something more specific, such as, "What can I do to increase my income by $25,000 in the next year?"

Now come up with 20 ideas. Tracy says let your mind flow freely. Write down every answer that pops into your head. It doesn't matter whether your idea seems realistic or unrealistic, intelligent or foolish, possible or impossible. Your job is to come up with 20.

The first few ideas might be logical—"work more hours" or "work faster," as anyone would expect. Maybe the next few ideas have more potential, such as "change jobs" or "start my own business," but those ideas would involve major career-changing shifts. Maybe you can create a new product or service, but that means being entrepreneurial minded.

As you would expect, the first few answers are easy or fairly easy, but finishing your list will be more difficult. You have to keep writing down ideas until you reach 20. Your last few ideas may sound totally ridiculous, and they very well could be. The beauty of the 20-Idea Method, Tracy says, is that very often a ridiculous answer triggers a breakthrough idea that might break a logjam and point you toward a path that could solve your problem— such as significantly increasing the amount of money you make each year.

After you have 20 ideas written down, study them. Is there one that seems reasonable enough to try at this time? You might have a gut feeling about this, and if so, then go with your instinct and take your idea to the next level.

I've been using a version of Tracy's mindstorming idea with great success over the years, incorporating the following exercise into several group-training sessions with my colleagues at work.

Here are the ground rules we use:

1. Everyone has to put away his or her smartphone during our mindstorming session.
2. Everyone is asked to come up with 20 ideas to increase sales, boost exposure, or find more clients.

Mindstorming can generate profound ideas, especially when the team is having difficulty overcoming a certain challenge. When everyone writes down 20 ideas or thoughts, a group of four could have up to 80 ideas or thoughts to work with, provided the ideas don't overlap. There is usually a handful of great ideas to explore.

If you try mindstorming, it's important you and your colleagues take your time. Mindstorming is not something you're going to get done in 5 minutes. Let the ideas flow. You don't want to stifle creativity or criticize ideas. Taming a wild idea is easier than invigorating a tame idea.

When all your responses are written down, discuss them and choose the top 15. Then look at the top 15 and decide whether one or two ideas are worth taking action on and implementing right away. A couple may fit those parameters, whereas others may be good long-term strategies.

The last thing to do is to decide which items stand the best chance for success and establish a timetable for taking action. You may have to combine ideas to find your solution, or you may have to schedule a follow-up meeting to analyze your top picks.

Once you've selected the best option, you can double the creative impact of the best idea by transferring it to the top of a new page and writing 20 more ideas for implementing it in your life or your business. You should be pleasantly surprised by how the 20-Idea Method results in an outpouring of creative ideas.

If you have been stuck and don't feel like you've been going anywhere, then try doing the 20-Idea Method. The big idea that has eluded you may suddenly appear.

SEEING RESULTS

I've proposed this mindstorming idea to some of the people I've coached in the past year. The president of a plastics company said he wanted to see $20 million in sales in the next 12 months. It had been bumping along between $13 million and $16 million for the past couple of years and seemed stuck.

I explained the concept of mindstorming and the 20-Idea Method and received a favorable response.

Then the president sat down with his four-person sales team, and each one was asked to come up with 20 ideas on how the company could go from $13 million to $20 million in sales. The ideas came gushing out:

- We can come up with a new product.
- We can go to new markets.
- We can attend the big trade convention in Las Vegas.
- We can expand to the East.
- We can expand to the South.
- We can open a manufacturing plant in Mexico.
- We can expand to the far West.

Their mindstorming sessions helped encourage innovative thinking, brought employees into the process, and led to many new ideas.

LAWYERS, ACCOUNTANTS, AND BANKERS (LAB) NIGHTS

At the investment bank where I work, we were looking for ways to increase our revenue. Like many investment banking firms, the global financial crisis affected us. Even though we were doing our best to meet one on one with lawyers, accountants, and bank executives—because they were our best referral sources—the investment banking deals were slow.

I called a meeting with three others in our firm and announced that we were going to conduct a mindstorming session. No idea would be too off-the-wall, I said. Also, no one could criticize the suggestions.

Some pretty wild ideas were thrown out for discussion. Then one of my colleagues said something that triggered an idea:

What if …

Here's the progression my thoughts took that afternoon. Our offices are located on the top floor of the Milwaukee Center Building in downtown Milwaukee. From the twenty-eighth story, we have awesome views from the floor-to-ceiling windows toward Lake Michigan and the Milwaukee skyline. When clients get off the elevator and step into our offices, there is definitely a wow factor.

"What if we hosted a wine-and-cheese reception for our network?" my colleague said. "We could invite a group of lawyers, a group of accountants, and a group of bankers and give everyone a chance to connect and talk about what they do."

We decided that it would be best to invite one law firm, one accounting office, and one bank to send five or six representatives. We even came up with a name for these events: LAB Nights, an acronym for lawyers, accountants, and bankers.

At the first LAB Night, executives and upper management from a local law firm, one of the Big Four accounting companies, and a major bank were invited to the twenty-eighth floor of the Milwaukee Center Building. Upon arrival, we asked each firm to appoint a captain and mingled with our guests.

After calling for everyone's attention and thanking the assembly for carving out time in their busy schedules, I said this: "We brought you together tonight because all of us assume we know what everyone does. We've been in the community so long, but what happens? Life changes, and our focus changes. For our lawyer friends, the regulatory climate has changed, so you are seeing new challenges with your clients. In the accounting world, your biggest challenge is implementing the complicated tax code that befuddles so many companies and clients. For our colleagues in banking, you have seen major regulatory changes in the wake of the 2008 mortgage meltdown, changing the way you do business.

"So, the purpose of tonight's gathering is to get to know each other a little bit better and see how we can work together because we're all in the referral business. So I'm going to ask each captain to talk about their company for a few minutes."

"I'll go first," I said. "As you know, I'm Joe Sweeney with Corporate Financial Advisors. We are a boutique, middle-market investment banking firm. We help people buy, sell, or recapitalize companies with a net value of between $10 million and $250 million. If you know somebody who wants to sell or recapitalize a company, give us a call."

Then the representatives from the law firm, accounting firm, and the bank all introduced themselves.

I said, "I'd like someone from your team to talk about a recent experience you've had or a deal you're working on. We don't you want to reveal clients and breach any confidentiality, but your story will give us a window into the challenges your company is facing in today's tight economy."

We heard one banking executive say, "We're currently doing an acquisition in China for a Midwestern-based company, and here are some of the challenges we're facing." Then he patiently walked everyone through some of his problems. We heard similar stories from the other firms.

We finished with a question-and-answer session. What was interesting about this was that as I looked around our conference room, I didn't see the four lawyers sticking together or the four accountants staying to themselves. I saw a lawyer, an accountant, and a banker huddling together, swapping stories and local business news. I felt good about what I was seeing. When would there ever be a reason for their paths to cross except at organized events like this?

Based on people's responses, our LAB Nights became an instant success, and it wouldn't have happened without mindstorming. The Wednesday night meetings became one of our most effective marketing plans that we executed.

FINAL THOUGHT

Finding innovative ways to solve business problems is key to staying relevant and nimble. The way we do business is constantly changing, so it is key to develop business solutions, identify new opportunities, and adapt swiftly to the changes in your industry constantly. Look at the turnover in Fortune 500 companies. Back in 1960, firms like American Can, Youngstown Sheet & Tube, and RCA held sway; more than 50 years later, only 75 of the Fortune 500 from the 1960s are still around and viable. By

2020, experts predict there will be 325 *new* companies on the Fortune 500.

Change is a natural phenomenon for business, for our careers, and for our lives.

Mindstorming is a great tool for helping you manage change and get going.

Joe's Recap

Mindstorming Ideas

- One of the best tools to get going is mindstorming, a technique that involves taking a question or conundrum and then brainstorming with others to provoke one of those aha! moments.
- Mindstorming is different from brainstorming. Mind-storming means coming up with 20 solutions to the difficult issue you're facing. The final ideas are often the best because more creative thoughts seem to come toward the end.
- Sort out the ideas, hash them out, and then either take a vote or make the decision on how to proceed. There's a good chance one of your mindstorming ideas will meet your original goal.

Exercises

1. Have you ever mindstormed with others and had great ideas come from the gathering? What results did you experience?

_____

_____

_____

Mindstorming to Manage Change

Goal: _____

List 20 ways to reach your goal
1.
2.
3.
4.
5.
6.
7.
8.
9.
10.
11.
12.
13.
14.
15.
16.
17.
18.
19.
20.

FIGURE 15.1 Mindstorming to Manage Change

(continued)

(continued)

2. Is your company facing a sticky problem that could be tackled with a mindstorming session? Would it be extremely difficult to come up with several solutions?

_____

_____

_____

3. Use the mindstorming exercise (Figure 15.1) from my 52-Week Winning Game Plan to creatively work through issues that your company is currently experiencing and then execute on these goals. Do the following:
- Select a goal with a minimum of three teammates.
- Have each person write down 20 ways to get there, for a total of 60.
- Do not allow any criticism of ideas.

4. After all the responses are done, discuss them all and choose the top 15. Look at the top 15 and decide whether there are one or two ideas that are worth taking action on and implementing right away. Execute a timetable and take action on the items every day for the next 15 days.

When you practice and complete this exercise, you will witness exponential growth.

CHAPTER 16

Differentiating Yourself with the Sweeney 22

Get Going

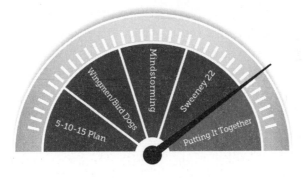

People don't care how much you know until they know how much you care.

—JOHN C. MAXWELL, author of more than 60 books, primarily focusing on leadership

When I spent time with the Navy SEALs, I learned one of the most important lessons in my life: Preparedness is the key to everything. The reason this is important in the military is that when dangerous missions and lives are on the line, you want to be locked down and ready for any scenario.

The business world isn't nearly as dangerous as what awaits the SEALs in faraway lands, but as I tell sales teams, being prepared means you never make a cold call or walk into a meeting cold. You want to learn as much as you can about whom you're dealing with and the company they're with *before* you tap out phone numbers. It's imperative that you acquire as much information as possible

193

before you introduce your product or service. Then you can cast yourself in the role of presenting solutions to their problems or pain. This concept circles back to the idea that the more you know about people, the better you can help them solve their problems. Remember, it's all about them and not about you.

You can't over prepare in these situations. Experts say the little things don't mean a lot in business, that it's more important to think big-picture stuff, but that sort of thinking is flat-out wrong. The little things mean *everything*. They're how you differentiate yourself.

So I have a few questions for you:

- Do you return phone calls, texts, or e-mails in a timely manner?
- Do you follow through when you say you're going to do something?
- Are you on time for meetings, or, if you're going to be late, call to explain your tardiness?

Never forget that when you're conducting business with another party, those on the other side of the table are consciously or subconsciously asking themselves three questions:

1. Do you really care for me, or are you trying to peddle a product?
2. Can you and your company really help me? Are you competent in what you're doing?
3. Can I trust you? Are the claims you're making reliable and reasonable?

You, on the other hand, have to be prepared to answer these three questions, whether they are verbalized or not. How can you do this? By finding something personable and doing something memorable. When you do those things, you will leave a lasting impression.

I'm always looking to find something personable and do something memorable with companies and individuals—from the CEOs to the junior account managers. That is one way you can differentiate yourself.

Let me give you a prime example.

Since the release of *Networking Is a Contact Sport* in 2010, I've tried to reinvent myself as a corporate speaker and trainer. I love getting up before audiences large and small and sharing my ideas about networking, leadership, and business development. I feel comfortable in this niche.

Corporate speaking is a highly competitive market. There are hundreds, if not thousands, of excellent speakers trying to get in the door. The weak economy of the past half dozen years has meant corporate belt-tightening, and one of the first things affected is outside speakers and continuing education.

So, how do I differentiate myself from others? By doing research that makes a lasting impression. Let me give you an example of what that looks like.

During a recent trip to South America, I was asked to speak to 400 leaders at General Electric's (GE) Experienced Commercial Leadership Program (ECLP) world leadership conference in Buenos Aires, Argentina. During my talk, I mentioned that you should never make a cold call, never walk into a meeting cold. You want to know who's there and know something about the people in the room.

I saw some eyes roll and a few people shift in their seats.

Pretending that I didn't notice, I continued: "I know what you're probably thinking: *You don't know our business, Sweeney. Because we make cold sales calls all the time*. I'm here to transform that type of thinking. Is Tom Smith here?"

Halfway toward the back of the auditorium, Tom Smith—I'm using a pseudonym—gingerly raised his hand. Tom looked to be in his late twenties, with close-cropped brown hair and wire-rimmed glasses.

"Tom, could you stand up?"

Tom looked momentarily bewildered.

"Would you mind coming to the front, Tom?"

Tom glanced at several hundred of his peers. I knew he was wondering what he was getting into. Nonetheless, he worked his way to the center aisle and made his way to the stage.

"Tom, you and I have never met, have we?"

"No, we haven't."

I turned to the audience. "You could go to GE's website and find out that Tom Smith graduated from Harvard Business School and works in GE Health Care.

"But let me tell you some things about Tom Smith that you don't know. He was born on May 18, 1979. He's one of four boys. His brothers' names are Mitch, Bill, and Sam. His father was a construction worker in upstate New York; his mother was a schoolteacher. His most memorable childhood experience happened when he was 13 and his brother Mitch sliced off three fingers at the wood factory. Tom went on to Princeton undergrad and Harvard for his MBA. At Princeton, he was a walk-on on the basketball team. He didn't play much, but he did score three points against Yale in 2001.

"He went on to marry Sarah Portman, whom he met here at GE. She's a nuclear physicist working in a different division. At this moment, she's in Tokyo at a conference.

"Tom says his most memorable adult experience was when their first baby was born. His favorite drink is a cosmopolitan. His favorite football player is Tom Brady of the New England Patriots. His nickname on the basketball court is LeBron because he's always talking trash when he plays in pickup games on Tuesday nights."

I hesitated for a moment to see how this was playing among Tom's peers, but they were hanging on every word. Also, Tom was beaming. By now, he was rather proud for being singled out.

I turned away from Tom and faced the audience. "You see where I'm going with this?" I continued. "So what did I just say about Tom? If I want to get close to Tom, I should know about his family and what his interests are. I should do my best to discover his background and who he is. *The more you know about someone, the better you can serve his or her needs*. As long as you're not overly intrusive—and I'll admit it's a fine line—people appreciate that you put the effort in to get know them better. Oh, yeah, what did I say about his favorite drink? I said he loves cosmopolitan martinis."

I reached underneath the lectern and handed him a bottle of Grey Goose vodka. The audience howled, and Tom's face broke out into a smile. "And what did I say about his favorite athlete? Here's an autographed football signed by Tom Brady."

I handed him an official NFL pigskin with Brady's autograph written large in black Sharpie ink.

Here's how I ended our interaction: "I know Tom loves reading great inspirational business books, and I just happen to have one of my favorites." I handed him a signed copy of *Networking Is a Contact Sport*.

"Everyone, give Tom a round of applause," I said as I watched him carry off his loot.

As expected, the first question I fielded in my question-and-answer session was this: "Joe, how did you find out all that information on Tom Smith?"

"The first thing I had to do was find someone who knew Tom," I began. "A good month before my departure to Buenos Aires, I reached out to my liaison at GE and told him what I was up to. He asked around and thought Tom would be a good subject for this experience. I asked this liaison some questions, some that he could answer and some he couldn't. He then offered to get in touch with his wife, Natalie, via e-mail and tell her what we were doing. She loved the idea and said she'd be glad to help out. I sent her a bunch of questions, which she answered, and I asked her to promise not to breathe a word to Tom."

What I did that morning in Buenos Aires was demonstrate how—by employing the Sweeney 22, which means asking 22 interesting questions about a person that go beyond the surface of the individual—you can get to know an individual and serve him or her better. It's not prying into private details but seeking out behind-the-scenes information that reveals something interesting or unique about the individual.

This usually means talking and e-mailing with an associate or fellow executive. Every time I've explained what I'm trying to do—create an experience and honor that person—people have enjoyed the exposure. I never reveal anything inappropriate. It's always a hit, and people comment on how helpful this exercise is.

Yes, the Sweeney 22 involves legwork as well an inquisitive mind and a willingness to scratch beneath the surface. But working through the 22 questions, which I share shortly, will likely net you the information you need. When you put that information to good use, you can make people feel special.

What I did in South America can be summed up in this statement, which I'm setting in boldface: **When you find out something personal and do something memorable, then you will make a lasting impression.** The quality of your personal and professional life is based upon the quality of your relationships, and the quality of those relationships is based upon the quality of your network, and your network is based upon your ability to connect with others.

The Sweeney 22 will help you develop rapport quickly and connect personally with prospects, clients, and coworkers, which is a key factor in differentiating your business, your products, and yourself from the competition.

Showing an Ability to Connect

Finding something personal and doing something memorable leave an indelible impression. Author and speaker Jack Canfield, who wrote the foreword for *Networking Is a Contact Sport,* frequents Ritz-Carlton hotels during his travels. Every time he checks in, there's a serving of chicken soup delivered to his room by the hotel staff, which is a thoughtful gesture for the man behind the *Chicken Soup for the Soul* series that has been a publishing phenomenon for the past 20 years.

Jeffrey Gitomer, another great speaker and trainer, also enjoys staying at Ritz-Carlton hotels when he's on the road. The staff knows that he's a sports memorabilia nut, so they'll do little things, such as having a baseball signed by the Ritz-Carlton staff waiting for him at check-in.

The Ritz-Carlton employees make their customer experience a priority and deliver that personal touch to their loyal customers.

THE SWEENEY 22

The Sweeney 22 is a great way to make an impression on others. In my 52-Week Winning Game Plan for business and personal development, I list 22 areas that can be mined for details. They are:

1. Birth date and location
2. Parents' names and occupations
3. Number of siblings
4. Names, sex, and order of siblings
5. Any nicknames of siblings
6. Memorable childhood experience
7. High school attended
8. Extracurricular activities in high school
9. College attended, major, and degree or graduate degree
10. Extracurricular activities in college or graduate school
11. Career timeline
12. Marital status
13. The names and ages of any children
14. Spouse's name and occupation
15. The hobbies or passions of the spouse or children
16. The person's own hobbies or passions
17. Most memorable adulthood experience
18. Favorite drink
19. Favorite food
20. Life's philosophy or mantra
21. Greatest life-changing moment
22. Any other unique information

You can feel free to add or substitute other background material, but the point is that it's critical to have information about those you're doing business with.

Finding out more about a person's interests gives you a chance to make an impression in a creative way. If you discover that a client or customer is a deer hunter or takes his or her family to the beaches in South Carolina every summer, then you might purchase a $12.95 subscription to *Field & Stream* or *Coastal Living* for that person. He or she is going to think of you the 12 times the magazine arrives that year.

One of the questions people often ask about the Sweeney 22 is this: *Joe, isn't this sort of creepy? Aren't you stalking?*

I don't think so. People reveal more information on Facebook. The more you know about a person, the better. If your job is to work on business opportunities that are beneficial to both sides, then information is a good thing. Showing more interest than simply asking, "How are the wife and kids?" conveys that you're willing to make the extra effort.

THE WOW FACTOR

You can take the Sweeney 22 to the next level by implementing the *wow factor*.

The wow factor is something that elicits astonishment and wonder, or something that shows others that you're aware of the interests or difficulties they are experiencing. A wow factor can even be coming up with problem-solving ideas. If any of those ideas is well received and works, then you know you have had an impact on that person.

Here are three questions to ask yourself when it comes to the wow factor:

1. Do you remember the last time you were wowed?
2. How did it make you feel? Explain what that moment meant to you.
3. When was the last time you wowed someone else?

If all of us can remember how great it felt to be wowed, why don't we make it a habit to do it more often for others? People remember you when you wow them, so to differentiate yourself with your clients and customers, think of doing something that would make them remember you.

People like to be remembered, and people liked to be wowed—or at least surprised by your business acumen. Here's an example of how the latter works. One time, I worked with a large law firm with 26 offices around the world in regard to its business development. This law firm asked me to help its members network better and improve their business development efforts as they were putting together a presentation that touted their attributes and ability to represent companies in corporate matters.

In the course of a conversation with one of the attorneys, he identified a $40 billion company they were seeking as a top client. As he continued speaking about this large company and how they'd love to engage it, I remembered seeing a news story in the morning paper in which the CEO of the $40 billion company stated that his number one challenge was growing his company's business from $40 billion to $60 billion in markets that it currently was not serving.

I mentioned that story to the attorney, which set a plan in motion to help their client grow his company to $60 billion by acquiring companies within markets it currently did not serve. Sometimes the best way to create a wow factor can be something as simple as staying informed about big trends or stories in your industry. The key is listening and reading carefully—in this case, the law firm was answering the challenge of the company before the company ever shared its challenges.

So, be thinking of doing something memorable and creating a wow factor. Even a small gesture—such as tucking a $10 gift card into a birthday card or a congratulatory note on a promotion—will make a lasting impression. Just the fact that you *did* something makes you stand out.

Joe's Recap

The Sweeney 22

- Before making a sales call or embarking on any type of business dealing, you need to figure out, ahead of time, what problems or pain that person may be experiencing. Then cast yourself in the role of presenting solutions to his or her problem or pain.

(continued)

(continued)

- Little gestures mean a lot. They are a way to serve others and help you differentiate yourself.
- Another way of differentiating yourself is by returning phone calls, texts, and e-mails in a timely manner. Being on time for meetings or calling if you're going to be late are also actions that speak volumes regarding your conscientiousness.
- When you're conducting business with another party, those on the other side of the table are consciously or subconsciously asking themselves three questions:
  1. Do you really care for me, or are you trying to peddle a product?
  2. Are you competent? Can you and your company really help me?
  3. Can I trust you? Are the claims you're making reliable and reasonable?
- The Sweeney 22, a questionnaire with 22 questions, will help you develop rapid rapport and connect personally and professionally with those you know in the business world.
- When using the Sweeney 22, you can add or substitute questions but the point is that doing business requires developing a relationship and expressing interest in those you interact with.
- Finding out more about a person gives you a chance to make an impression in a creative way that doesn't cost a whole lot of money.

Exercise

1. Make copies of the Sweeney 22 (Figure 16.1) and try to fill in at least five items for individuals with whom you work, such as clients, suppliers, coworkers, or even potential employers.

The Sweeney 22 to learn more about a person

1. Birthdate and location _____

2. Parents' names and occupations _____

3. Number of siblings _____

4. Names, sex and order of siblings _____

5. Any nicknames of siblings _____

6. Memorable childhood experience _____

7. High school attended _____

8. Extracurricular activities in high school _____

9. College attended/graduate degrees/majors _____

10. Extracurricular activities in college/grad school _____

11. Career timeline _____

12. Marital status _____

13. Kids' names and ages _____

14. Spouse's name and occupation _____

15. Spouse/kids' hobbies/passions _____

16. His or her hobbies/passions _____

17. Most memorable adulthood experience _____

18. Favorite drink _____

19. Favorite food _____

20. Life's philosophy/mantra _____

21. Greatest life-changing moment _____

22. Any other unique information _____

FIGURE 16.1   The Sweeney 22

CHAPTER 17

Putting It All Together

Get Going

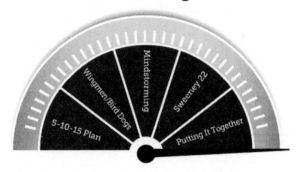

When you *start* with an attitude of serving others instead of looking for what you can get out of the encounter, amazing things can and will happen, as illustrated by the following story about one of my dearest friends—Sister Camille Kliebhan of the order of the Sisters of St. Francis of Assisi.

Sister Camille Kliebhan has served in a number of high-profile administrative and academic positions at Cardinal Stritch University near my hometown of Fox Point. I'm privileged to call her a close friend.

Sister Camille has been at Cardinal Stritch in one capacity or another nearly 60 years. She was a trailblazer of sorts, becoming one of the first three women to be admitted to the downtown Rotary Club in 1987. She must have made a great impression because a few years later she was asked to become the first female president of the local Rotary Club.

Several notable things happened between 1974 and 1991 when Sister Camille was president of Cardinal Stritch. She presided over a 400 percent increase in student enrollment and oversaw the development of new programs in nursing, business management, educational leadership, and public communication.

In the early 80s, Cardinal Stritch developed a Reading Clinic, which was a social outreach program centered on the promotion of reading instruction, and it just so happened that the Second Lady of the United States—Barbara Bush, wife of then U.S. Vice President George H. W. Bush—had made literacy her platform. One thing led to another, and Barbara Bush flew to Milwaukee to visit the Reading Clinic and talk with instructors and clinicians.

Mrs. Bush and Sister Camille hit it off, so when the Cardinal Stritch president began casting about for a commencement speaker to address the Class of '81, she knew just whom to invite. Barbara Bush immediately said yes to Sister's invitation to speak at the commencement and receive an honorary degree.

I had met Sister Camille when a group of us started a free week-long basketball camp back in the late 1980s and was looking for a gym. She offered use of the school gymnasium at no cost. As Humphrey Bogart said at the end of the classic film *Casablanca*, "I think this is the beginning of a beautiful friendship."

A few years ago, Tami and I were invited to a social event with Sister Camille. Before dinner was served, we got into a deep conversation, which led me to ask this question: "Tell me, Sister. If you could do anything in your life before you die, what would it be?"

"I would like to have lunch with First Lady Barbara Bush and her husband, President Bush," she said.

"Why them?" I inquired.

She thought for a moment and then described how 30 years earlier, in 1981, Barbara Bush had given the commencement talk at Cardinal Stritch and received an honorary degree. Sister Camille mentioned that she stayed in occasional contact with Barbara Bush. Now that she was 88 years old, she'd been thinking about getting her affairs in order. "I turned a lot of my files and correspondence over to the historian at Cardinal Stritch University, including personal letters from Barbara Bush. I've been reflecting on Barbara and how much I miss her … "

Sister Camille's voice trailed off, no doubt because she was replaying warm memories in her mind.

I thumped the table. "Well, Sister, we're going to figure out how to do this, first thing tomorrow morning!"

When I woke up Monday morning, I said to myself, *Oh, my God, what did I commit myself to? Trying to put together a lunch with the First Lady and the forty-first president of the United States? Where do I start?*

I remembered an acquaintance, John McConnell, a former attorney who had also been a speechwriter for President George W. Bush and Vice President Dick Cheney. I'd made some interesting connections over the years through the practice of trying to follow through on the small things. After contacting John, he gave me an e-mail address for Hutton Heston, the personal assistant to Barbara Bush.

I wrote a letter telling the story about Sister Camille and how she met Barbara Bush and describing how Sister wished to have lunch with her and her husband.

The response from Heston was golden: "Barbara has fond memories of Sister, and she'd be open to the possibility of doing lunch."

I proposed that Sister Camille could fly to the President's hometown of Houston, Texas. Was there a date that worked for everyone?

Hutton Heston wrote back, "The Bushes aren't in Houston during the summer. They are in Kennebunkport."

I recalled seeing their seaside home on the rugged Maine coast in news reports during President Bush's administration, but flying from Milwaukee to Kennebunkport? Not wanting to take the chance that we'd miss a connecting flight from Boston or some airport in the Northeast, we needed to come up with a plan B.

What could I do to solve this conundrum? Then I remembered Chris Doerr, who owned Sterling Aviation, a charter aircraft company. We had been good business associates as well as friends.

I reached out to Chris and asked for a favor. "Can you help me out with a special trip I'm planning?" I inquired. "I need to go out East for an important lunch."

"Must be quite a lunch," Chris replied. "What's the deal?"

I told him the whole story, about President Bush and Barbara agreeing to have lunch with Sister at their home in Kennebunkport.

"Well, if you're going to see the President, you might want to consider flying in a Challenger," he said. Chris explained how a Challenger is a $30 million business jet that costs in the range of $8,000 an hour, so a trip out there and back would be $40,000 to $50,000.

That was a little more than I was planning to pay. Maybe I could work a discount.

"So, Chris, what kind of deal can you cut me?" I joked.

"If you take me as your wingman, I'll fly you and Sister Camille for free."

"You're on," I said.

On September 7, 2011, Chris, Sister, and I settled into the over-sized leather seats in the business jet and enjoyed the pleasant trip eastbound. We landed at a nearby commuter airport, where a shuttle van drove us to the oceanfront presidential compound.

As we approached the front door, I wondered whether a valet or housekeeper would greet us. Instead, Barbara Bush opened the front door, a wide smile visible on her famous face.

"Welcome Sister!" she exclaimed with arms wide open. She and Sister Camille hugged like two long-lost friends reuniting after many years.

Waiting just inside the front door was President Bush.

We were ushered into their lovely home and given a tour of the first floor. There were pictures of the Bush family everywhere—on walls, the stairwell, and every table. Many were with world leaders, such as Russian President Vladimir Putin or German Chancellor Angela Merkel, but others were family snapshots of weddings and graduations like you'd see in any home.

FIGURE 17.1   **Sister Camille Kliebhan and First Lady Barbara Bush in the dining room at Kennebunkport, looking like two sorority sisters**

"Would anyone like something to drink?" Mrs. Bush asked, ever the gracious host.

"An iced tea would be wonderful," I said.

The First Lady frowned. "Well, the president doesn't like drinking alone," she said. "Could I interest you in a glass of white wine before lunch?"

I drink very little, especially during the daylight hours.

"Why, I'd love a glass, Missus—"

"It's Barbara," she said.

"Right . . . Barbara."

When we sat down in their living room, I mentioned that I had read their son's memoir, *Decision Points,* in which he described the critical decisions that shaped his presidency. "Those letters you sent to your son, the commander-in-chief, when American military forces entered Iraq really hit me emotionally," I said. "I was in tears. I showed them to my wife, and she cried. So did my kids. We all cried."

At that moment, I saw President Bush tear up as a housekeeper announced that lunch was being served. When I took a seat next to President Bush at a rectangular dining table, I wondered who else had sat in my chair—kings, queens, presidents, or senators? We were quickly served the main course, which was a lobster salad. Very apropos for the Pine State.

The First Lady asked Sister Camille if she would say grace before the meal. If you've ever heard Sister Camille pray in public, then you know how heartfelt and personal her prayers can be. I was seated next to President Bush and was holding his hand as Sister Camille prayed that the Lord would bless and protect His faithful servants, George and Barbara Bush, who had done so much good ... and then I peeked—and saw a tear running down the President's face.

I started choking up. The moment was getting to me. I heard Chris make a muffled sound.

When Sister Camille had finished her earthly eloquence, Barbara Bush looked surprised. "What's everyone crying for?" she asked.

The lunchtime conversation was fascinating, ranging from current and past politics to Sister Camille discussing the state of higher education. President Bush had a certain twinkle in his eyes. When he talked to us, his eyes sparkled, and he occasionally winked at one of us. I think the President was trying to bond with us, as in *Hey, you're okay. I like you guys.*

Ice cream was served as dessert.

There was one last question. "Barbara, how long have you and George been married?" I asked.

"Sixty-six years," she replied. She stopped, and it was one of those pleasant pauses. "You know, he might be the finest husband and best human being I've ever met in my life."

Once again, emotion overtook me. They were so sweet. George had this look of admiration where you knew these two connected. It reminded me of the film *On Golden Pond* with Henry Fonda and Katharine Hepburn, where they had that look between each other. You could tell how much they were in love with each other.

We said our goodbyes, hugged each other, and headed back to the airport for the return flight. Sister Camille beamed while she sipped a celebratory gin martini just after takeoff.

As we were flying westward at 39,000 feet, I announced, "I have a confession to make."

Chris and Sister Camille gave me their undivided attention.

I reached into my left pocket and showed them a paper napkin with the presidential seal. When I had been handed the glass of white wine before lunch, I had discreetly slipped the paper napkin into my pocket.

"I guess it's time for me to come clean as well," Chris said. "I did the same thing." And he pulled a presidential napkin out of his pocket, too.

Sister Camille chuckled and opened up her purse. "I think I got you all beat," she said, and she showed us a paper towel with the Walker's Point logo on it.

What memories we made and what laughs we shared! But as I reflect, what happened that day in Kennebunkport was never about having lunch with the First Lady and the President of the United States. It started with this simple question: *How can I help Sister Camille pull off this dream of hers?*

Once I started down the path of helping others, invisible hands came out of nowhere to guide us. Everything that I had practiced and talked about over the years—asking good questions, looking for ways to serve others, and following through on the small things—came together in this rich experience.

Over the course of 30 years, I've made it a practice to develop and act on these habits, which have given me clarity and the freedom to get going. The result is that I've tried to help others go places in life they never expected, which leads me to this conclusion:

> If you can help other people get what they want, you can do things you never imagined possible.

FIGURE 17.2   In gratitude for sharing a most memorable day with President George H. W. Bush and First Lady Barbara Bush

Conclusion

25 Key Takeaways

1. To get *clear*, get *quiet*. Take 15 minutes a day in the classroom of silence.
2. If you can create a big enough *why,* the *how* will take care of itself.
3. To find your life mission, combine your *passions* and *strengths* to serve others.
4. If you want to get clear, understand the three most common basic needs of others. They are the need to belong to something bigger than ourselves, the need to love and to be loved, and the need to know that our life has meaning.
5. The best way to keep balance in life is to become aware of all the plates spinning in our lives. Manage each segment of your life in an organized and focused manner.
6. Understanding the elements of product differentiation, you can become more highly desirable, uniquely obtainable, and economically irresistible.
7. It is important to create your ideal day on paper and do your best to live it each day.
8. Designing your ideal day can help you to design an ideal week, ideal month, ideal year, and ideal life.
9. Creating a *have, do, and be* list will make your life fun and adventuresome and will always give you things to look forward to.

10. To become free really means looking at your self-limiting thoughts.
11. You can become truly free only when you take 100 percent responsibility for everything in your life.
12. Practicing the 200-year rule will help you become more grateful for the daily gifts you receive.
13. Finding your Zone of Genius will help you create game changers in your work and life.
14. In many business situations, alignment is more critical than strategy.
15. Success in business and in life is more about managing paradoxes than about doing simple how-tos.
16. Your habits are great predictors of what your life will become. If you really want to change your life, change your habits.
17. You haven't lived a perfect day until you have done something for another person who has no way of ever repaying you.
18. Increase your energy dramatically by focusing on people, places, and events that excite you.
19. If you can get the proper mind-set about money, you will prosper. Thinking about scarcity leads to more scarcity.
20. It is important to create a positive system at work and at home. The 5/10/15 plan is a tool that can get you on track.
21. To make a real difference in people's lives, find something *personal* and then do something *memorable*.
22. Touch trumps technology.
23. It is critical to surround yourself with your own board of directors (wingmen and wingwomen) to get direction and clarity.
24. Mindstorming will help you and your group work creatively to solve your challenges.
25. When you help other people get what they want in life, you will be surprised at how your needs are met as well.

Joe Sweeney's Recommended Reading List

A Nation of Takers: America's Entitlement Epidemic	Nicholas Eberstadt
A New Purpose: Redefining Money, Family, Work, Retirement, and Success	Ken Dychtwald and Daniel J. Kadlec
Body for Life: 12 Weeks to Mental and Physical Strength	Bill Phillips and Michael D'Orso
Eat That Frog! 21 Great Ways to Stop Procrastinating and Get More Done in Less Time	Brian Tracy
Entrepreneurial DNA: The Breakthrough Discovery That Aligns Your Business to Your Unique Strengths	Joe Abraham
Excuses Begone! How to Change Lifelong, Self-Defeating Thinking Habits	Wayne W. Dyer
Falling Upward: A Spirituality for the Two Halves of Life	Richard Rohr
Halftime: Moving from Success to Significance	Bob Buford
How to Win Friends & Influence People	Dale Carnegie
Killing Lincoln: The Shocking Assassination that Changed America Forever	Bill O'Reilly and Martin Dugard
Lone Survivor: The Eyewitness Account of Operation Redwing and the Lost Heroes of SEAL Team 10	Marcus Luttrell
McDonald's: Behind the Arches	John F. Love
Networking Is a Contact Sport	Joe Sweeney

Off Balance: Getting Beyond the Work-Life Balance Myth to Personal and Professional Satisfaction	Matthew Kelly
Outliers: The Story of Success	Malcolm Gladwell
Spiritual Economics: The Principles and Process of True Prosperity	Eric Butterworth
Start with Why: How Great Leaders Inspire Everyone to Take Action	Simon Sinek
StrengthsFinder 2.0	Tom Rath
Success Built to Last: Creating a Life That Matters	Jerry Porras, Stewart Emery, and Mark Thompson
Swim with the Sharks Without Being Eaten Alive	Harvey B. Mackay
Team of Rivals: The Political Genius of Abraham Lincoln	Doris Kearns Goodwin
The Big Leap: Conquer Your Hidden Fear and Take Life to the Next Level	Gay Hendricks
The Biology of Belief: Unleashing the Power of Consciousness, Matter, & Miracles	Bruce H. Lipton
The Birth Order Book: Why You Are the Way You Are	Kevin Leman
The Blue Zones: Lessons for Living Longer From the People Who've Lived the Longest	Dan Buettner
The Compound Effect	Darren Hardy
The Energy Bus: 10 Rules to Fuel Your Life, Work, and Team with Positive Energy	Jon Gordon

The Go-Giver: A Little Story About a Powerful Business Idea	Bob Burg and John David Mann
The Greatest Generation	Tom Brokaw
The Greatest Miracle in the World	Og Mandino
The Hero with a Thousand Faces	Joseph Campbell
The Millionaire Next Door: The Surprising Secrets of America's Wealthy	Thomas J. Stanley and William D. Danko
The New Gold Standard	Joseph Michelli
The Passion Test: The Effortless Path to Discovering Your Life Purpose	Janet Bray Attwood and Chris Attwood
The Power of Habit: Why We Do What We Do in Life and Business	Charles Duhigg
The Power of Myth	Joseph Campbell
The Rhythm of Life: Living Every Day with Passion and Purpose	Matthew Kelly
The Sales Bible: The Ultimate Sales Resource	Jeffrey Gitomer
The 7 Habits of Highly Effective People	Stephen R. Covey
The Success Principles: How to Get from Where You Are to Where You Want to Be	Jack Canfield
The Wisdom of Wooden: My Century On and Off the Court	John Wooden
The World Is Flat	Thomas Friedman
Think and Grow Rich	Napoleon Hill
Today Matters: 12 Daily Practices to Guarantee Tomorrow's Success	John C. Maxwell

Undaunted Courage: Meriwether Lewis, Thomas Jefferson, and the Opening of the American West	Stephen E. Ambrose
Virus of the Mind: The New Science of the Meme	Richard Brodie
What They Don't Teach You at Harvard Business School: Notes from a Street-Smart Executive	Mark H. McCormack
Wishes Fulfilled: Mastering the Art of Manifesting	Wayne Dyer
Younger Next Year: Live Strong, Fit, and Sexy—Until You're 80 and Beyond	Chris Crowley and Henry S. Lodge

Notes

CHAPTER 1   WHEN IT COMES TO GETTING CLEAR, FIRST GET QUIET

1. Schulte, Brigid. *Overwhelmed: Work, Love, and Play When No One Has the Time*. New York: Sarah Crichton Books, 2014.
2. Comaford, Christine, "Got Inner Peace? 5 Ways To Get It NOW," www .forbes.com/sites/christinecomaford/2012/04/04/got-inner-peace-5-ways-to-get-it-now.
3. Dyer, Wayne W. *Wishes Fulfilled: Mastering the Art of Manifesting*. Carlsbad, CA: Hay House, 2012.

CHAPTER 3   GET CLEAR WITH YOUR LIFE MISSION

1. Hughes, John, Michael Chinich, Matthew Broderick, Alan Ruck, and Mia Sara. *Ferris Bueller's Day Off*. Hollywood: Paramount Pictures, 1986. Video-cassette (VHS).
2. Attwood, Janet Bray, and Chris Attwood. *The Passion Test: The Effortless Path to Discovering Your Life Purpose*. Reprint, New York: Plume, 2008.

CHAPTER 5   CLARITY IN DIFFERENTIATING YOURSELF

1. Dyer, Wayne W. *Excuses Begone! How to Change Lifelong, Self-Defeating Thinking Habits*. 4th ed. Carlsbad, CA: Hay House, 2011.

CHAPTER 6   GETTING CLEAR BY CREATING YOUR IDEAL DAY AND IDEAL LIFE

1. Buford, Bob. *Halftime: Moving from Success to Significance*. Rev. ed. Grand Rapids, MI: Zondervan, 2008.

SECTION II   GET FREE

1. Emme. "Meme." In *Urban Dictionary*. Last modified December 10, 2003. http://www.urbandictionary.com/define.php?term=meme.

CHAPTER 7   GET FREE BY TAKING 100 PERCENT RESPONSIBILITY

1. Freud, Sigmund. *Civilization and Its Discontents*. W.W. Norton & Company, reprint ed., 2010.
2. Boetcker, William John Henry. *Lincoln on Limitations*. The William J. H. Manuscript Collection. Princeton Theological Seminary Library.
3. Louis C.K. Comedy Central. January 1, 2011, www.cc.com/video-clips/1myllo/stand-up-louis-ck--the-miracle-of-flight.
4. Moorehead, Bob. "The Paradox of Our Age." In *Words Aptly Spoken*, 197–198. Kirkland, WA: Overlake, 1995.

CHAPTER 8   YOUR PERSPECTIVE DETERMINES YOUR FREEDOM

1. Kelly, Matthew. *The Rhythm of Life: Living Every Day with Passion and Purpose*. Reprint, New York: Touchstone, 2005.
2. Brett, Regina. "Regina Brett's 45 Life Lessons and 5 to Grow On." *Plain Dealer* (Cleveland, OH), May 28, 2006. http://www.cleveland.com/brett/blog/index.ssf/2006/05/regina_bretts_45_life_lessons.html.

CHAPTER 9   FREEDOM AND THE ZAP CONCEPT: ZONES, ALIGNMENT, AND PARADOXES

1. Hendricks, Gay. *The Big Leap: Conquer Your Hidden Fear and Take Life to the Next Level*. New York: HarperOne, 2010.

CHAPTER 10   HABITS AND GETTING FREE

1. Buettner, Dan. *The Blue Zones: 9 Lessons for Living Longer From the People Who've Lived the Longest*. Reprint, Washington, DC: National Geographic Society, 2012.

2. Covey, Stephen R. *The 7 Habits of Highly Effective People*. Simon & Schuster, anniversary edition, 2013.

3. World Health Organization. "Obesity and Overweight." Last modified May 2014. http://www.who.int/mediacentre/factsheets/fs311/en/.

4. eMarketer. "Digital Set to Surpass TV in Time Spent with US Media: Mobile Helps Propel Digital Time Spent." August 1, 2013. http://www.emarketer .com/Article/Digital-Set-Surpass-TV-Time-Spent-with-US-Media/1010096.

CHAPTER 12   GET FREE WITH YOUR MONEY

1. Ramsey, Dave. *The Total Money Makeover: A Proven Plan for Financial Fitness*. 3rd ed. Nashville: Thomas Nelson, 2009.

CHAPTER 15   MINDSTORMING IDEAS

1. Tracy, Brian. *No Excuses! The Power of Self-Discipline*. New York: Vanguard Press, 2011.

About the Author

Joe Sweeney is the founder of Pay It Forward Enterprises, a speaking, training, and coaching enterprise that helps companies and individuals move the needle in their personal and professional lives.

He was the former president and shareholder of Corporate Financial Advisors and is currently a strategic advisor to CFA, a middle-market investment banking firm in Milwaukee, Wisconsin. CFA specializes in providing merger and acquisition advisory services, capital sourcing, exit planning, and general corporate advisory services. Joe is also an active private equity investor in several businesses.

Throughout the years, Joe has built several businesses by combining his love of business and his passion for sports. He has a wealth of hands-on experience. Joe has owned and operated four manufacturing companies and has more than three decades of experiences in the business and sports worlds.

Before acquiring an equity position with Corporate Financial Advisors, Joe founded and was president of SMG, a sports management firm that specialized in assisting and representing coaches and athletes. Clients included Green Bay Packers quarterback and three-time NFL Most Valuable Player Brett Favre. Joe was also president of the Wisconsin Sports Authority and has served on 28 boards of directors over the past 30 years. He received his Bachelor of Arts degree from Saint Mary's University of Minnesota and his Master of Business Administration degree from the University of Notre Dame.

Based on the success of his first book, *Networking Is a Contact Sport* (BenBella, 2010), Joe has given hundreds of keynote addresses and workshops over the past few years to a variety of businesses, corporations, military branches, and universities, such as Northwestern Mutual, General Electric, Wells Fargo, Merrill Lynch, ManpowerGroup, CUNA Mutual, Minnesota Wild NHL hockey team, Morgan Stanley, Travelers Insurance, UBS, and the Navy SEALs.

Additionally, Joe serves in the capacity of advisor to a number of privately held businesses nationwide, and he is a private investor in several Midwest-based companies. He has used his 30 years of business experience to become a master networker, coach, and mentor.

Joe and his wife, Tami, are the parents of four adult children and make their home in Fox Point, Wisconsin.

Joe's website is www.JoeSweeney.com.

Mike Yorkey, who collaborated with Joe Sweeney on the writing of *Networking Is a Contact Sport,* is the author or coauthor of more than 85 books with more than 2 million copies in print. Mike and his wife, Nicole, are the parents of two adult children and make their home in Encinitas, California.

Mike's website is www.mikeyorkey.com.

INVITE JOE SWEENEY TO SPEAK TO YOUR COMPANY OR ORGANIZATION

Joe Sweeney is a dynamic speaker and trainer who encourages and teaches others what it means to move the needle in today's business climate as well as about how networking can grow your business, expand your influence, and make life richer and more meaningful.

If you or your company would like to book Joe Sweeney, contact him at:

Joe Sweeney

Pay Forward Enterprises

111 E. Kilbourn Avenue, Suite 2800

Milwaukee, WI 53202

(414) 431-4886

Joe@JoeSweeney.com

For bulk purchases of *Moving the Needle* or *Networking Is a Contact Sport*, please contact Pay Forward Enterprises directly. For more information, visit www.JoeSweeney.com.

The Winning Game Plan

The Winning Game Plan is a business and personal development system created by Joe Sweeney and is available in 8-, 16- or 52-week programs to assist you and your team in moving the needle to grow your business while obtaining your personal life goals to discuss with Joe. This program is a two-way relationship in which your team examines their goals, habits, and systems; Joe will provide the support, accountability, perspective, and the resources for the achievement of these goals.

This program is designed to help you and your team stay engaged and improve performance. It requires a commitment to homework and a willingness to implement business and life changes.

For more information on the Winning Game Plan, visit www.JoeSweeney.com.

Index